The

Rosetta

A Handbook for Transcendent Experience by Integrating the Metaphors of God

By

Mark Dobson

First published by AuthorHouse 06/01/04

ISBN: 1-4184-5866-X (e-book)
ISBN: 1-4184-2806-X (Paperback)

Library of Congress Control Number: 2004104938

Printed in the United States of America
Bloomington, IN

This book is printed on acid free paper.

Cover art: "Galaxy," by Cathy Dobson, oil on canvas 48" X 48".
Other works may be viewed at *www.absolutearts.com*.

March, 2011

Hope you love this too, Tom.

Love,
Donna

Contents

Illustrations by Noah Hosburgh:

Time Spent In the Present Moment, 9
Thrown-ness, 14
Subliminal Music of Life, 32
I Choose, I Chose, 46
Monks Listening To Water, 81

Introduction

Six Faiths, One God

A stone tablet, upon which were chiseled messages in several ancient languages, was found in 1799, in Rosetta, Egypt, and has unlocked cultures once lost in pre-history by providing a side by side translation.

Likewise, the six major religions on the earth, Judaism, Christianity, Islam, Hinduism, Taoism, and Buddhism, as well as hundreds of other religious practices and philosophies, speak in different languages, using different metaphors, to convey the same revelations about who and what we are. And in each faith are many who have been guided to live in compassion, reverence, mindfulness, and love by these universal, perennial truths.

Dharma Versus Dogma

In each of these religions are also millions of adherents who completely miss the fundamentals because they are focusing literally on these metaphors, which only exist to convey a reality of the Oneness in which we all have our being. As each faith employs parables to teach the laws of God and the universe, the literal-minded see great differences between the faiths, much like comparing the skin on several pointing fingers, instead of turning to face the one direction they all are pointing.

Those known as fundamentalists would be the ones so far from the fundamentals as to try to enforce your fixation on the fingertip, and persecute any who would attempt to see where it points.

When scriptures are setting you free, making you feel at peace, expanded, and connected to a continuous immortality, you can call them Torah, Dharma, Gospel. When these **same words** are used narrowly to limit or reduce you, confine, define, or frighten you, they become authoritarian, knuckle-whacking dogma.

Perennial Philosophy

Though the images and parables differ, their essence is a Perennial Philosophy. As described by Aldous Huxley, it's the central mystical theme which each of these faiths has sought to express. The "Word of God" has been written not only in Hebrew, Aramaic, Greek, Chinese, Sanskrit, and Arabic, but in every tongue, on paper, parchment and tablets, "on the subway walls and tenement halls," and shouted from mountain, rooftop, and car-stereo.

Each religion contains **mystical elements, in which the personal experience of direct knowledge is senior to mere belief,** with similarities beyond coincidence. The Hebrew *tzimtzum* (concealment and contraction of the primordial Divine light), the Buddhist *animitta* (seeing through the outer form), the Arabic *al haqq* (the Real, the Divine Ground or Unity of Allah), and the Hindu *Brahman* (God) and *maya* (form or illusion), are **describing the same transcendent nature of reality** as the Judeo-Christian metaphor of Father and Son, and the Taoist teaching of the Un-namable and the named. These are brought together in this handbook as the One and the Many.

Kabala, (Jewish mysticism) teaches that the Torah, proclaimed to the Jews in the barren desert of Mt. Sinai, was without echo, and continues to penetrate every cell and every grain of sand in all the languages of the world. Thus the Perennial Philosophy, planted in the heart of each of the Many in the wilderness of the physical world, has been preserved and expressed with the local flavors of India, China, and Israel as intricate systems of knowledge. Each faith offers a set of proven guidelines for living in harmony with the One, a world-view that if understood and practiced brings the happiness of a sanctified life.

Every person would do well to read at least one basic work of each of these six religions, with the understanding that each scripture uses metaphors to communicate ultimate truths beyond language. And just as the Rosetta Stone answered many questions on the interpretation of ancient writings, a comparative survey of faiths will not only further peace and tolerance, but will produce a deeper vision and a greater likelihood of a personal transcendent experience of the One, the most important event in your life: to at least momentarily pass beyond human limits and experience existence above and independent of materiality.

Take this simple test to determine if you believe in God.

1. Is all of existence "one"? (Is there a One, from which separation is ultimately impossible, outside of which nothing can be, the laws of which pervade all of existence?)

2. Is all of existence "alive"? (Does the One have consciousness both as a whole Being and in every single part?)

If you answered yes to both questions, then you do believe in God. If you thought you were an atheist, you were merely disagreeing with certain of the metaphors of God, but not with the One that these phrases were attempting to convey.

If you answered no to either or both of the questions, then you do not believe in God. If you thought you were a believer, you were merely believing in metaphors on a literal level, but not in the One towards which these images point.

The Paradox of the Observant

The leaders, the holy ones, the highly observant in every religion, from Baptist to Scientologist, the ones who walk the walk, in whom you would find a living example of their teachings, whose lives reflect the dedication, the forgiveness, the compassion, the devotion, humility, and loving kindness evident in their sacred writings, the individuals we would wish to emulate in our own lives, are the ones most likely to have absolute certainty that their faith is the only true path, and that all who would hope for salvation would ultimately have to accept it. Can this paradox be overcome?

I believe in all the scriptures that God has revealed. We have our own works and you have yours. Let there be no argument between us. God will bring us all together. (Koran 42:15)

BOOK ONE: PRECEPTS

The Rim of the Grand Canyon

Stretching endlessly beyond the railing is a sight of color and depth that cannot fail to free the mind from every imaginable concern, and awaken the higher being waiting within. Standing before the staggering presentation of objects and distances, your sense of self sustains a total makeover.

Now imagine a coin-operated binocular upon a metal stand directed out over the rim of the Grand Canyon. Standing alongside to accept your quarter is a Catholic priest. An elaborate crucifix decorates the pedestal.

Just twenty feet further along the path is an identical metal stand, this binocular decorated with the Tai Chi symbol. Collecting quarters is a Taoist priest in golden robe inviting you to come view the fabulous Grand Canyon.

Another twenty feet finds another same binocular, but adorned in mosaic with the star and crescent moon. A turbaned sheikh beckons you to view the one true canyon, and you start to wonder how different these lenses really are.

As you lift your gaze, the unimaginable vastness takes your breath, and the little path along the rim is occupied by one clergyman after another, each one with a lens, each one urging you to see it his way.

As we go for a little jog down the lane we meet a rabbi, a Buddhist monk, various Protestant ministers, a Hindu priest, a Wiccan, a Bahai, several shamen, and others, each with a bona fide, properly labeled, orthodox, coin-operated binocular.

And all the while, the canyon vista is so overwhelmingly present, dominating each moment with form, depth, and beauty so expansive, that it would require us to have veiled ourselves in many layers of dark shroud and deep ignorance, pretending there is no canyon at all, before we could find in these lenses any purpose at all.

This indeed is what we've done. We have deeply endarkened our awareness, and therefore all of these binoculars are of utmost value.

The Supreme Ultimate

Ultimate Truth cannot be contained in words, described, defined, or fixed by code or formula. And yet words have connected us to our higher Self since before the recorded history of our alleged solidity. Every culture, every tribe of humans found words of wisdom which opened the inner eye to see through the attractive distractions known as the world. These holy words might be known as the Law, the Good News, or the Whispers of the Elders. Stories, parables, poems, songs, and sacred puzzles, pulling back the curtains of our unknowing, are the Metaphors of God.

In the Tibetan Book of the Dead we learn that **"objectively nothing exists outside the Unity of Mind."** This same teaching is a senior and basic precept in each of the six major faiths (see Book Four, List One), which have their own unique metaphorical statements of it, as well as workable religious philosophies that follow logically and naturally from this one premise.

Precepts One through Six below can be found both implicitly and explicitly in the mystical thinking of such diverse sources as Kabala, Course in Miracles, the Tao Te Ching, the Bhagavad Gita, the Dhammapada, the Koran, and the Bible. We will look at some implications of these six perpetual axioms, and then in the following sections expand towards a unified presentation of the world's religions as offering us a state of mind that is both prior to and senior to a solid, objective reality.

Precept One: The One is always and forever becoming the Many. The One is also known as the Universe, the All, Brahman, the Tao, (the Way), the Infinite, the Subtle Origin, the Great Spirit, Allah, the Father, Ha-Shem, (the Name), and God. The "becoming the Many" is also known as the Separation, the Creation, the Big Bang, the Manifestation, the Exile.

Precept Two: The Many are always and forever becoming the One. The Many are also known as the world, people, the ten-thousand things, you, me, individual souls, the Son, every blade of grass, every wave on the ocean, and every grain of sand. The "becoming the One" is also known as the Return, the Communion, the Revelation, the Atonement, the Redemption.

Precept Three: The entire One is accessible in each of the many. Because the One is a Quality rather than a quantity, its totality is simultaneously everywhere. This accounts for all miracles.

Precept Four: The One is alive and is the only aliveness there is. All apparent forms and organisms are of the same living essence, and not even separate, except by our subjective assignment of boundaries.

Precept Five: The One is conscious and is the only consciousness there is. The individuality, the ego, personal karma, and uniqueness of viewpoint are all barriers to consciousness, much like a sprinkler head is a barrier to a flow of water, to aim the flow in certain directions, in unique patterns and personalities. There is one original flow, one water, one consciousness.

Precept Six: There is nothing else but the One. Right perception would reveal that even the metaphorical sprinkler head is made of nothing but the same water as flows through it.

The Alleged Physical Universe

"God is pure and ever One, and ever one they are in God." (Bhagavad Gita). If this is so, then the One and the Many and their mutual becomings comprise the totality of existence. By definition, nothing else can possibly exist, nor could there be any condition other than Life, also known as God. Relative conditions such as "life" and "death," the drama of individual lives, and biological or planetary systems, have existence only in our subjective interpretations. All of the following observations, portraits, and poems are presented as necessarily proceeding from the perennial precepts of One-ness.

Matter: Life does not and did not emerge from matter. Matter is one of the infinity of subjective observations that emerge from Life. Molecules, atoms and finer particles; galaxies, black holes, and quasars; body organs, blood, and nerves do not exist "out there" or anywhere except where they serve to reflect to us the continuity of our beliefs of the moment.

Energy: All energy and emotion derive directly from apparent differences, (all reducible to the fundamental difference, the apparent difference between the One and the Many), as viewed from any viewpoint amongst the Many. Light, sound, and sensation, in ranges of subtlety, are sought and found, created and experienced by the Many through comparison (applied relativity).

Space: We re-create a sense of distance every moment. One definition of space can be: the game-board upon which we move our game-piece.

Time: Linear understandings of religious and scientific metaphors place the One at "the Beginning," earlier in "time," than the Many. But time itself is a subjective viewpoint, a product of Precepts One and Two. The Big Bang did not happen in the past. The One is always and forever becoming the Many. The Big Bang and time itself are metaphors we invented to define our world.

"Time Spent In the Present Moment" c. 2004 Noah Hosburgh, hand-cut screen print

Though we continue to create a physical universe subconsciously, these functions can potentially be done in full awareness, but only to a very limited degree as long as we insist on remaining human. Part of the definition of human is a voluntary unknowingness of the One, and a subjugation to physical laws by our acceptance of physical bodies as identities.

It is only which, so to speak, "direction" we turn our eyes which determines whether the One is becoming the Many or the Many becoming the One for us (and as us) at that moment. The mission of the Many is to traverse and experience the entire Land of Expression between the Many and the One, in both directions, elevating all of the Many to their ultimate nature of the One, while forwarding the treasure of Oneness to every atom. We do this armed with limited perspectives, but capable of fully accessing the One at any point.

BOOK TWO: METAPHORS

Fact and Metaphor

A metaphor can be defined as an implicit comparison. We use this figure of speech because it more accurately communicates for us a reality that cannot be captured with mere facts. To say, "Bill's thoughtless behavior has led to damaging and embarrassing consequences," is not nearly as satisfying as "He's a total asshole." That's metaphor, doing its job. To say, "When Cindy walks into the room I become happy," does not convey the depth of the subjective experience like "She is a cool, refreshing breeze."

What is the truth we wish to communicate in each example? Keats said, "Beauty is Truth, Truth beauty…that is all ye need to know." In the above messages the metaphors are, of course, not **literally** true. Cindy is not a short-lived weather phenomenon, and Bill is not a remote body-part. So, are these lies? No. My point is that a more profoundly accurate communication comes forth in the beauty of the implicit comparison.

In a TV interview, the writer of the history book on which the movie, "The Gangs of New York," was based, said that certain alterations of the facts, liberties taken by the film maker, resulted in the real story coming across. In other words, **fiction communicated more truth than factual history.** The unfolding of drama in the screenplay helped the viewer get the flavor of the period on a level that penetrated the surface to the place where understanding could be reached, even though names, dates, and events were fabricated.

The metaphor is possibly the most important literary device available, the most responsible for elevating written communications to masterpieces. But even beyond this noble feat, it is the only way to describe the Indescribable. How else can we begin to speak of that which is infinite, that which is far greater than the literal reach of our languages?

"Though there can be no name for it, I have called it the Way of Life." (Tao Te Ching 25). Attempting to dissect this statement on a literal level, we might think of the Supreme Ultimate Reality as some sort of road, or perhaps a recipe or set of principles. But I hope you will find that this metaphor is pointing to the same Living Endlessness which some call God.

History and Myth

Our many stories of miracles, heroic journeys, and divine beings walking the earth are known as myths. Similar to a metaphor, a myth is an entire narrative in which characters and events represent aspects of our own inner world. Many long established stories are virtually the same in distant lands: God taking on human form, princesses mating with wild creatures, resurrections from the grave. How can this be? Did someone in pre-history steal a writer's ideas twelve thousand miles away?

No, these myths have endured in widely separated cultures because they tell of the struggles within our psyches between the forces we humans must balance or overcome. Such a story may involve a diamond ring in one version and a golden fleece in another, a journey by ship or by flying horse. The original "writer" encoded it in our DNA and even more subtle levels of our being, and the mythic journey, should we choose to accept it, is towards self-knowledge, attainment of our own highest nature, and one-ness with the Source of life.

History selects a specific story and seeks to solidify it, erecting a monument to finite events, confirming times and places upon a well-defined game-board. It asserts what exactly occurred at each point in the chain of cause and effect. This may actually have some value in the handling of business in the workaday world and one's sense of national citizenship, as history offers an acceptable explanation of our progress in these specific arenas.

Myths, on the other hand, are accounts of the adventures we must face regardless of the country or the economy. Whether we find them in the writings of Moses or of Homer, these are the stories that are true everywhere, all the time, and especially if we see beyond the particulars to the pervasive truths. Loaded with different combinations of universal and local metaphors, they aim at the same target, the honest examination of the state of our souls.

Literal and Literate

Why can't King David make up his mind? Is the Lord a judge or a shepherd, a light or a rock? Silly question, because we are already aware that all of these metaphors aim at a greatness, an everything-ness beyond all words. But can we realize that so too "Lord" and "Father" and whatever other thousands of words and phrases, epithets and praises with which we attempt to share our acknowledgement of the One, are metaphors? Only then are we sufficiently **literate** to reach the underlying one-ness of all the world's faiths.

"I and the Father are One" (John 10:30). Does this mean that only this person is made of pure divinity while the rest are made of clay? Is he the Father's only child? Or is he stating the perennial mystical truth about the reality of the Many and the One that every religion addresses as its major, central theme?

Literal thinking is the kind that's important in following instructions in the material world, and is an indispensable survival tool on such a playing-field. You don't want your surgeon getting metaphorical with your organs.

But likewise, the **literal** interpretation of religious metaphors is one of the greatest sources of war and intolerance. One group chants, "Hare Krishna!" (Praise God!), and another proclaims, "Allah hu akbar!" (God is great!), and another, "Boruch Ha-Shem!" (Blessed is God!). You would think they'd get along better than they do.

It is actually by means of a literal interpretation of myths that we create the solidified version known as history. It takes some force to fix the metaphors into finite permanence. This is how we end up living in a world that's been defined for us by others, in which pre-conditioned responses to symbols relieve us of any need to personally experience the present moment.

By regaining our literacy, in this case an ability to recognize metaphor, to receive the stronger message it carries, and to find and discard any literal assumptions we've accepted in the study and pursuit of divinity, we might leave behind the confining habit of seeing what we're supposed to see, and enter an expanded realm in which every mundane activity is exalted to mythic endeavor, and adventure lurks at every step.

Jesus and Magdalena

This story is true. Woe to he who would say to you "It is just a myth", for he has thus condemned himself to the shallow puddles of the literal and forsaken the ocean of Truth, which awaits the literate who recognize that which is eternal. Indeed! This is Myth! Far senior to the factual! Much more than the mere historical! It is now and forever.

Magdalena first saw the young man, Yeshu ben Yoseif, in the market as he and a fellow student of the Torah delivered a wooden chest to a wealthy merchant. The older man was very pleased with the work and uttered many praises, even comparing it to the Ark of the Covenant! The two scholars were invited to sit upon a carpet. Loaves of bread and a bowl of humus were brought forth, and wine was poured into wooden goblets from a clay jar.

"She most certainly did cast her gaze upon you, my fortunate fellow class-dodger," said Ari to his bright-eyed companion, "but alas she isn't one of us."

Yeshu nodded and stole another glance towards the girl, Magdalena, across the plaza. Her back was turned but she felt his eyes and took a pretext to reach, to stretch. "It is Ha-Shem's command that we be fruitful and multiply, and lest we forget, He presents to us such creatures of the desert to distract us from our studies. Shall we examine her wares?"

..thrown into being - like a wave - my life brings with it an inevitable death - yet, with the ability to take a consciously active part in my existence - i possess an immeasurable potential energy...

"Thrown-ness" c. 2004 Noah Hosburgh, woodcut

Universal Metaphors of God

The metaphors of God are as numerous as the thoughts of all the poets and prophets. As long as a spark of life twinkles, it shall proclaim a bottomless reservoir of inspired communion between the Many and the One. Some words and phrases have served worldwide for millennia in mankind's attempt at a literary leap from the natural to the Supernatural, and offer both positive and negative imagery for perspectives on our place in the divine order.

Light, darkness, fire, water, words, music, love.

The tree, the ocean, the road, the king, the river, the curtain, the wall, the rock, the mountain, the desert, the well.

Up and down, father and son, mother and child, earth and sky, heaven and hell, day and night, the sun and moon.

These are some of the images that have transmitted the meaning of humanity and divinity, but also have led us to the illiteracy of image-worship, fundamentalism, and fear.

In the following metaphorical verses, think of examples of how **literal** interpretations would merely solidify the hopeful and fearful images while missing the point, and compare these with **literate** understanding in which the actual meanings are imparted.

The Metaphor of Fire

Like a flame we rise towards oneness in our prayers and meditations, studies and retreats, seeking the Supreme Ultimate Reality at the core of our being:

"I see thy face as a sacred fire that gives light and life to the whole universe in the splendor of a vast offering." (Bhagavad Gita 11:19)

"That which is bright rises twice. The image of fire. Thus the great man, by perpetuating this brightness, illumines the four quarters of the world." (I Ching 30)

"You know that I would be a liar if I were to say to you we couldn't get much higher. Come on baby light my fire." (Jim Morrison)

It is like a conflagrant hell, that which awaits us if we fail to master our human desires:

"Behold, the Lord will come with fire, and with his chariots like a whirlwind, to render his anger with fury, and his rebuke with flames of fire." (Isaiah 66:15)

"Better to swallow a flaming, red-hot ball of iron than to live an uncontrolled life at the expense of others." (Dhammapada 308)

"I fell into a burning ring of fire. I went down, down, down, and the flames grew higher, and it burned, burned, burned, this ring of fire." (Johnny Cash)

The Metaphor of Water

Like water, divinity descends into the details of daily existence, to refresh every dry corner:

"The supreme good is like water, which nourishes all things without trying to. It is content with the low places that people disdain." (Tao Te Ching 8)

"He shall come down like rain upon the mown grass as showers that water the earth" (Psalms 72:6)

"God made a song when the world was new. Water's laughter sings it through. O, wizard of changes, teach me the lesson of flowing." (Robin Williamson)

Caught in the flow, with lost sense of purpose, though we are surrounded by holiness, we yet cannot drink of its blessings:

"The currents of his passion-based thoughts carry him away, that man of wrong views for whom the streams of craving flowing towards pleasure are strong." (Dhammapada 339)

"If one gets down almost to the water, and the rope does not go all the way, or the jug breaks, it brings misfortune." (I Ching 48)

"Water of love, deep in the ground, but there ain't no water here to be found." (Mark Knopfler)

The Metaphor of the Tree

Like the tree, we span from earth to heaven:

"Its root is firm and its branches are in the sky; it yields its fruit in every season by God's leave. God speaks in parables to men so that they may take heed." (Koran 14:26)

"And he shall be like a tree planted by the rivers of water, that bringeth forth his fruit in his season; his leaf also shall not wither; and whatsoever he doeth shall prosper." (Psalms 1:3)

"In the church made of living trees entwined, green and dapple golden trees enshrined us." (Licorice McKechnie)

As physical entities, like the tree, we are rooted in corporeal reality:

"And when the woman saw that the tree was good for food and that it was a delight to the eyes, a tree to be desired to make one wise, she took of the fruit thereof and did eat. And she gave also unto her husband with her, and he did eat. And the eyes of them both were opened, and they knew that they were naked." (Genesis 3:6)

"Its branches spread from earth to heaven, and the powers of nature give them life. Its buds are the pleasures of the senses. Far down below, its roots stretch into the world of men, binding a mortal through selfish actions." (Bhagavad Gita 15:2)

"Well, she's flying so freely in the sky. Hey, look at me, Lord, I'm rooted like a tree." (Richie Havens)

The Metaphor of Words

The spoken word brings the entire creation from a state of concealment and potential to full manifestation:

"In the beginning was the Word, and the Word was with God, and the Word was God." (John 1:1)

"The unnamable is the eternally real. Naming is the origin of all particular things." (Tao Te Ching 1)

"There's a blaze of light in every word. It doesn't matter which you heard, the holy or the broken hallelujah." (Leonard Cohen)

In seeking separate ego-glory, we misunderstand each other's words, and see all our works crumble:

"Therefore was the name of it called Babel, because the Lord did there confound the language of all the earth, and from thence did the Lord scatter them abroad upon the face of all the earth. (Genesis 11:9)

"Better than a thousand meaningless words is one word of sense, which brings the listener peace." (Dhammapada 100)

"I've grown tired of your words, a linguistic form that can meaningfully be spoken in isolation, conversation, expression, a promise, a sigh, in short a lie." (Madonna)

The Metaphor of Darkness

In the darkness of pure potential is the source of all the manifest world:

"Tao and its many manifestations arise from the same source: subtle wonder within mysterious darkness. This is the beginning of all understanding." (Tao Te Ching 1)

"And the people stood afar off, and Moses drew near unto the thick darkness where God was." (Exodus 20:21)

"Don't go turning on your light babe, I'm on the dark side of the road." (Bob Dylan)

In darkness, the absence of God's light, we are lost:

"The wicked move in the darkness as hidden as arrows in the night." (Dhammapada 304)

"Darkness upon darkness. If he stretches out his hand he can scarcely see it. Indeed the man from whom God withholds his light shall find no light at all." (Koran 24:40)

"We sang dirges in the dark the day the music died." (Don McLean)

The Metaphor of Light

We seek enlightenment that we may see what is real:

"I am the light of the world: he that followeth me shall not walk in darkness, but shall have the light of life." (John 8:12)

"He is the Light of all lights which shines beyond all darkness. It is vision, the end of vision, to be reached by vision, dwelling in the heart of all. (Bhagavad Gita 13:17)

"My eye was single and my body was filled with light. And the light that I was was the light that I saw by. And the light that I saw by was the light that I was. (Mike Heron)

Too much light at once, beyond our human limits, only brings more darkness:

"The god of this world hath blinded the minds of them which believe not, lest the light of the glorious gospel of Christ, the image of God, should shine unto them. (2 Corinthians 4:4)

"How difficult thou art to see! But I see thee as fire, as the sun, blinding, incomprehensible." (Bhagavad Gita 11:17)

"Blinded by the light: Mama always told me not to look into the sights of the sun." (Bruce Springsteen)

The Metaphor of the Mother and Child

Her nurturing embrace enfolds us in the protection of Oneness:

"The Tao is called the Great Mother, empty yet inexhaustible, it gives birth to infinite worlds." (Tao Te Ching 6)

"As one whom his mother comforteth, so will I comfort you, and ye shall be comforted in Jerusalem, and when ye see this, your heart shall rejoice." (Isaiah 66:13)

"I said mother I'm frightened, the thunder and lightning, I'll never get through this alone. She said I'll be with you, my shawl wrapped around you, my hand on your head when you go." (Leonard Cohen)

She is the ravenous goddess who swallows her offspring:

"And upon her forehead was a name written: Mystery, Babylon the Great, the Mother of Harlots and Abominations of the Earth, and I saw the woman drunken with the blood of the saints." (Revelation 17:5)

"At the sight of your shape stupendous, full of mouths and eyes, feet, thighs, and bellies, terrible with fangs, I and all the worlds tremble in fear." (Bhagavad Gita 11:23)

"Motherly love is just the thing for you. Your mother's gonna love you till you don't know what to do. We can love you till you have a heart attack. You'd best believe that's true. We'll bite your neck and scratch your back till you don't know what to do." (Frank Zappa)

The Metaphor of the Father and Son

The Creator extends in all directions, and his presence is imprinted on all of his creation.

"The Lord hath said unto me, Thou art my Son, this day have I begotten thee." (Psalms 2:7)

"I am the Father of this universe, and even the Source of the Father." (Bhagavad Gita 9:17)

"Father of night, father of day, father who taketh the darkness away, father who teacheth the bird to fly, builder of rainbows up in the sky." (Bob Dylan)

He is the masculine force of fear and vengeance:

"And I will execute great vengeance upon them with furious rebukes; and they shall know that I am the Lord, when I shall lay my vengeance upon them." (Ezekiel 25:17)

"Father, ruler of the family; act as father; paternal, patriarchal, authoritative rule. The ideogram: hand and rod, the chastising father." (I Ching 37)

"Father, father, we don't need to escalate. You see, war is not the answer, for only love can conquer hate." (Al Cleveland, Marvin Gaye, Renaldo Benson)

The Metaphor of the Ocean

Only in the vast Oneness, does each wave and droplet have its reality:

"Even as all waters flow into the ocean, but the ocean never overflows, even so the sage feels desires but he is ever one in his infinite peace." (Bhagavad Gita 2:70)

"When you know that the body is merely the foam on the crest of a wave, unreal as a mirage, you will break the flowery arrows of craving." (Dhammapada 46)

"I turned around and the water was closing all around, like a glove, like the love that had finally, finally found me. Then I knew in the crystalline knowledge of You." (Stevie Nicks)

When your essential nature is reclaimed by its Source, your separate identity is drowned:

"And the waters returned, and covered the chariots and the horsemen, even all the host of Pharaoh that went in after them into the sea, there remained not so much as one of them." (Exodus 14:28)

"For thou hadst cast me into the deep, in the midst of the seas, and the floods compassed me about; all thy billows and thy waves passed over me. Then I said, I am cast out of thy sight." (Jonah 2:3)

"Drowning in a sea of love where everyone would love to drown." (Stevie Nicks)

The Metaphor of Music

The Uni-Verse, the one living song in which we sing, is composed of all the notes and vast infinite silences: the complete array of all the Many, and greater still, the un-manifest endlessness of the One:

"Thy statutes have been my songs in the house of my pilgrimage." (Psalms 119:54)

" I am the Brihat songs of all songs in the Vedic Hymns. I am the Gayatri of all measures in verse." (Bhagavad Gita 10:35)

"When the music's over, turn out the lights, for the music is your special friend. Dance on fire as it intends. Music is your only friend, until the end. (Jim Morrison)

Out of sync with the great Song, we hear only distant dreams or meaningless cacophony:

"Poets are followed by erring men. Behold how aimlessly they rove in every valley, preaching what they never practice." (Koran 26:226)

"And the songs of the temple shall be howlings in that day, saith the Lord God: there shall be many dead bodies in every place. They shall cast them forth with silence. (Amos 8:3)

"What's that? Hawaiian noises? Bangin' on the bongos like a chimpanzee. That ain't workin.' (Mark Knopfler)

The Metaphor of Love

It is our nature to extend love, and thereby does the One further the creation:

"Only by love can men see me, and know me, and come unto me." (Bhagavad Gita 11:54)

"The Lord hath appeared of old unto me, saying, Yea, I have loved thee with an everlasting love: therefore with loving kindness have I drawn thee." (Jeremiah 31:3)

"All you need is love. Love is all you need." (John Lennon and Paul McCartney)

Misdirected to specific objects, love becomes idol worship, fear, and pain:

"For the love of money is the root of all evil: which while some coveted after, they have erred from the faith, and pierced themselves through with many sorrows." (1 Timothy 6:10)

"You have chosen idols instead of God, but your love of them will last only in this nether life." (Koran 29:25)

"One man come in the name of love, one man come and go. One man come, he to justify, one man to overthrow. In the name of love, what more in the name of love?" (Bono)

The Metaphor of the Chosen People

A People in whom righteousness prevails will be granted furtherance in the journey to the One:

"Blessed is the nation whose God is the Lord, and the people whom he hath chosen for his own inheritance." (Psalms 33:12)

"So the last shall be first and the first last: for many be called, but few chosen." (Matthew 20:16)

"Well, I dreamed I saw the silver space ships flying in the yellow haze of the sun. There were children crying and colors flying all around the chosen ones. All in a dream, all in a dream the loading had begun. They were flying Mother Nature's silver seed to a new home in the sun." (Neil Young)

An arrogant, divisive People will wander through many confusions and quarrels:

"But God hath chosen the foolish to confound the wise; and God hath chosen the weak to confound the mighty." (1 Corinthians 1:27)

"Such is God's guidance: He bestows it upon whom he will. But he whom God confounds shall have none to guide him." (Koran 39:25)

"Loyalty to their kind, they cannot tolerate our minds. Loyalty to our kind, we cannot tolerate their obstructions." (Paul Kantner)

The Tree of Knowledge

The eating of the apple represents the "beginning" of human "history". Prior to our making that choice, is total communion with the One, a state of direct Knowledge, in which the true nature of everything as an expression of the One is experienced in every thought and action. To eat of the Tree of the Knowledge of Good and Evil, is not a step upwards towards Knowledge in any sense. It is a step down from Knowledge to knowledge-of-good-and-evil, on a scale in which the next level down is total confusion:

Knowledge (Communion, Heaven)
Knowledge of Good and Evil
Total Confusion (Hell)

In the expulsion from the Garden of Eden, God is not saying, "I am now going to punish you for taking a forbidden fruit." God is saying, "Now that you've chosen a world of relative values, comparisons, and judgments about everything you see, here are some coming attractions which are the inevitable components of such a world: suffering, pain, old age, and death."

In eating the apple of Eden, we chose to view a non-existent dark side, providing an apparent balance of good and evil. We consider ourselves tiny enough that all the movements of the Many can provide us realistic drama, in which the impossibility of becoming lost seems real, in which God can be forgotten in our unknowingness of our own identity. The illusion of a long journey looms in our self-imagined land of darkness.

Tower of Babel

"And the whole earth was of one language and of one speech...Come, let us build us a city, and a tower, with its top in heaven, and let us make us a name; lest we be scattered abroad upon the face of the whole earth." *(Genesis 11)*

Our very action of commencing such a project ensured that we would indeed be dispersed. The tower to God's abode, like the earlier similar apple, only appealed to the ego. And like the Nazis in the Indiana Jones parables, who tried to capture and harness the Holy Grail and the Ark of the Covenant as weapons, the ego (in biblical Hebrew, *the satan*) is the part of us seeking to *"make us a name,"* to establish its throne outside of the One, and seduce us into believing this could possibly succeed.

So we think we can enlist the powers of Oneness to assist us in enforcing further separation! And faster than the fall of a TV evangelist caught in Las Vegas, we're no longer *"of one language and one speech."* We squint and grope at the metaphors of God, argue about literal and historical details, and punish those who will not accept our set of facts.

Surfing

A sport that doesn't require any competition or score keeping, in which the pure pleasure of activity is its own reward, surfing offers us a guiding metaphor of daily living. While we cannot dictate each next "wave," we must choose to ride some as best we can, and some we can let pass us by. But it's in **how** we ride the waves we pick, that the pursuit of excellence for its own sake is fully in our hands. We are, all of us, surfers. Every moment brings your next wave. **Come, he said, I will make you surfers of Life.**

I Am a Drop

I am a drop of water splashed forth from the Ocean. In this separate life I may collide with other droplets or particles, and may even spawn other droplets that bear the mark of my own unique aquacity. Part of me in the distant future will fall back into the sea, while another part rises to the clouds to fall upon the earth and nourish other life forms, before ultimately returning to the same Ocean from whence I sprung. There is much to think about during this brief illusion of my existence.

Jesus and Magdalena

The human soul is located nowhere and everywhere, its secrets told by music, myth, and metaphor, the language of God.

Few have known of the musical prowess of the young man Yeshu ben Yoseif. Without formal training, he yet could channel a mesmerizing series of melodic intimacies on the oud and the bazouki, as dozens of Jewish and Arab youths would participate outside of town. The girl Magdalena would attend, chanting Assyrian verses while slapping a tambourine as she twirled under a billion stars in the desert night.

Jamming

It is only a small part of God that is impinged upon the physical world, and yet God can be reached through the myriad doorways of silence between any two beats. Only a small part of **you** is impinged upon the physical world. The remainder is with God, but unnoticed.

While the One Song is far greater than the capacity of human ears, any mutual activity shared by two or more beings in cooperative motion puts us into harmony with the One. All our communications are of the same nature as the infinite living Song, but by music itself we can knowingly link with our Source. Its finer vibration allows us to speak more truthfully, using the language of melody, harmony, and rhythm, to share our experiences amongst the Many in our journey to the One.

The word "jam" comes from Ja, a Biblical name of God. To jam is to reunite with God. Three people with sufficient agreement on rhythm and melody, can make of any song a prayer that dissolves the boundaries of their separate identities. In the domain of simultaneously playing and being played, they reach Oneness.

On the island of Jamaica dwell the "Jam-makin" people. Using the form known as reggae, they realize God through their music. In the devotional attitude of the reggae masters, even the most worldly of pop lyrics, TV themes, or silly jingles become hymns of worship.

Every life encounter can be received as a jam-offering, an invitation to participate in rhythm and harmony, to bring your fellow beings into knowing participation in the great Song.

Subliminal Music of Life c. 2004 Noah Hosburgh, hand-cut screen print

BOOK THREE: CONSTELLATIONS

We connect the dots, we **constellate** incessantly to provide ourselves our personal experience of the Many. This is a new verb. The noun "constellation" now has the additional meaning of "the act of choosing, from amongst the infinity of living stardust, specific finite realities." You organize your own world-view, your pre-conscious assumptions of what is real, of what is worthy of your notice. And then you find your perceptions confirm these categories of experience. But they are no less subjective than picking out three stars and calling them "Orion's Belt." Time is but a theory to explain the apparent sequences in our choices of which dots to connect.

The Prayer of Constellation

Out of the infinite living stardust from which I constellate my life, may I find and fashion the pathways back to Infinity. May I refrain from selective constellation of others, that I not prejudicially choose to connect an arbitrary handful of stars, ignoring the dazzling array before me, to unjustly portray a weak or lacking being. May I always seek to constellate truthfully, to see the radiance of my fellow beings even when it is momentarily obscured from my limited view by a minute cluster of dark stars, which may indeed prove to be my own.

"In the beginning was the Word, and the Word was with God, and the Word was God." (John 1:1)

Tell us, John, mystical prophet and apostle, what is it you are talking about?

The Alleged World

Nothing is pre-ordained. Everything already is. The endless and dazzling array of the Many, all the infinite potential combinations, exist in pristine glory and absolute goodness, regardless of our constellation thereof. And in our constellating we divide the infinite living Word into past and future, and assign sequences and call them Time.

The alleged world is merely your mirror, and the mirror can trick you, as left appears right, and what is within you seems to be outside. From infinite living stardust which some call God, you constellate the characters who populate your dreams and nightmares, looking outward to find that which is inward.

All the people in your world receive from you the breath of life. Yes, it is you who keep them alive, keep them vibrant and beautiful as the important players in the drama of your journey. They will rise to their roles as you direct your awareness their way.

And they will be as you would have them be, as you need them to be to fulfill the destinies of your personal adventures on route to your own glories and crucifixions, to your prized victories and your cherished failures. To solidify the game-board on which you move your little piece, you firm up the foul-lines and the rules, re-defining where you're going and where you've been, according to your meanings of the moment. Though you walk through a valley of shadows, it is all you and only you. The One, manifested as the Many, is infinite living stardust. The constellations, the connections, are the mythical and metaphorical meanings that only you assign.

The Out of Body Experience

When the family sits down to play a board game, do you forget yourself to the extent that you become the little piece you move around with each roll of the dice?

Is it a sudden shock to realize that you're sitting at a table with friends and family, enjoying a game in loving companionship? Does that piece, that little hat or car, become for a while your whole existence, that it's all you conceive that you are?

Probably not. But in the game known as Life, that is how far interiorized you have become.

When you play a board game, you remain out-of-the-piece, out of your designated game-body. You don't get so far down into it that the conceptual boundaries of your identity are a one-inch plastic droplet.

But in your living of your life you have gone so deeply into the game that you've forgotten that the border of the tiny piece you move about, the skin around your body, is not the limit of the space you really occupy.

There is a greater Table at which you sit, from which you play this Game of Life for loving companionship and joy.

Jesus and Magdalena

Let he who doth resist the myth, who doth favor the fact, today hold tightly to his tongue, for these words are Truth universal, as are the personalities of which they speak, facets of revelation, aspects of the manifestation of divinity in the world.

Waking together in the desert, the young lovers greeted and blessed the new day. As mourning doves and nature's day-shift began clocking in, Yeshu's breathing rose and fell with the rhythms of the Assyrian songs of praise fluttering from the voluptuous lips of his dark skinned soul-mate. He bobbed and bowed, reciting his morning prayers, thankful for the beauty and love of this girl who so wonderfully widened his knowledge of Ha-Shem, bringing him into holy communion with the Creator and all of Creation.

Today was a school day. For the boy this meant Torah study, with much discussion of application to daily life. His arguments with teachers were artful and inspired. He bore no ill will for their neglect of direct revelation, confinement to the letter of scripture, as they grow old and tired. The Romans install the High Priests, and the rabbis have to answer to these collaborators. In the face of forced mediocrity, it was no simple task to open all eyes to Light, all ears to the Word of God all around them, but he vowed he would remain young forever.

For the girl Magdalena this would be a day of accompanying tribal mothers in routine chores, as all the girls would watch and listen and copy and add their own personal flavors in their education as desert goddesses who could perform every task from erecting a tent, to bathing a camel, to making a man howl at the moon in devotional desire.

Putting away his tefillin, Yeshu watched her apply paint and glitter above her eyes, and gloss to her lips, watched as she brushed a series of ravens in ink all the way up her legs. Magdalena laughed and jangled her ankle bracelets. "Don't you have to get to class already?"

Jesus and His Teacher, Rabbi Yehoshua Ben Peracchia

Yoshka, Yoshka, still with the metaphors? Again with the parables! Is it not a material fact that with miracles and a mighty hand the Lord delivered us from Egypt?
Yes, Rabbi, it is a fact in the physical universe that the seas did part and great wonders did unfold.
But?
But the material world is merely one of the many in which we dwell. And the majesty of Ha-Shem's work resounds throughout the realms. It is only by metaphor that we awaken to our infinity and our ultimate one-ness with

the Creator, as did the Lord's beloved servant, our ancient grandfather, David, the king.

And what say you, Yoshka, to our sages who teach us that the physical world is the highest of the worlds, the jewel, the final product towards which all the intermediate dimensions were aimed, the crown of creation?

I say, learned Rabbi, that yes, only by living in the material world can we experience the full glory of Ha-Shem's radiant brilliance, which is denied to the angels who are relegated solely to the spiritual. But by metaphor we live knowingly, above the beasts and our own beastly natures, sharing in the glory of every ray of light as it emanates from the Father to us, the Son.

Tell me Yoshka, what is the Crown of Creation?

It is, Rabbi, as we have spoken, the physical world, the manifestation of Ha-Shem's light. But of course, Man, created on the sixth day, would be the crown of the crown. And then it would follow that Woman, the next step, the masterpiece, is the jewel of the crown. And then the final creation, fashioned in the wilderness of Sinai to forever bring the Light into the world, would be the true Crown of Creation, the Bride of Ha-Shem, the Jewish People.

So then, Yoshka, tell me this, what then are you doing fooling around with an Arab girlfriend?

Revered Rabbi, your humble student does not fool around. Every song and every breath are dedicated to Ha-Shem, who guides me where He will, and reveals to me what He will. Perhaps Magdalena has a Jewish soul, blessed by Abraham, father of the Arabs and the Jews, for she is my soul mate.

The Inverted Sun Diagram

Each sun-ray extends into the Living Void, and is jagged to provide more contact with the Infinite. And each jag is so jagged, a plethora of jags. And there are inlets, lakes, and fjords until every single speck of the finite world is in perpetual contact with Infinity.

As we sleepwalk through the material world, heads wound tightly with the yarn of darkness, unconscious, drunk, and stupid, we stumble onto a path to the Infinite, for there is no place else, and we've never left, but we walk these paths to awaken.

And awakenings occur on every path. And God is found on every point of every path. Are you looking for God? Well you can't miss Him (Her/It)! Seek ye the Infinite? It is right where you are, at every point of contact. There is nothing else.

In every activity, God is accessible, at every level of skill. An Olympic skier can finish fourth place in the world and say, "I wasn't in sync, I just didn't have it today," while a vacationer on the intermediate slope, who'll never be near any kind of tournament, can happily proclaim, "Exhilarating run! Divine joy! Perfect speed! Oneness with nature!"

Is There Life On Other Planets?

The earth-centric beliefs of pre-1500's man have been deemed primitive with the widening acceptance of the constellational metaphor of the earth orbiting the sun. We view from selected spots in an endless and intricate matrix of livingness which some call God. There is nothing **but** life on this planet, other planets, moons, stars, asteroids, comets, cosmic dust, and the supposed spaces between.

And the nature of our constellations change. Theoretically it is possible we all could one day, by the powers invested in us, grant beingness to space men. Many already have done so, and neither the Air Force nor the psychiatrists can persuade them otherwise. Perhaps popular demand will render the parables of Star Trek our new playing field on the material plane. And perhaps it already has, whether in the distant past or an alternate present.

For such realities are possible if they serve the furtherance of the mythic journey to self knowledge. Perhaps these extra-terrestrials are necessary to our regaining the Kingdom of the One, otherwise we will surely not bother to mock them up.

Was the primitive man right about the center of the universe? He had no idea of how right he was, though the answers existed implicitly in the Vedas, the Tao, and Kabala since pre-history. Your subjective experience, as you lay in bed at night, of being transported by benevolent beings to inter-galactic centers of knowledge, is one of your constellational rights.

The Stubbed Toe

If you are a vast and infinite being, immortal and godly, then this physical world is only a small part of your existence. Just as a stubbed toe draws all your attention to the area of pain, so too the small part of you impinged upon the material world is the part you notice most.

There Is Only One Moment

There is only one moment, the moment of Now, in which the One entertains the thought of separation into Many, and the Many laugh as they rush to rejoin that from which it is impossible to have ever departed.

The worlds we see with our eyes, worlds of time and space, struggle and death, are the visions we, in the addictive contemplation of "real" separation, perchance to dream. How deeply into hell can I extend my dream world? How convincingly can I pretend to be beyond the reach of that which I never left?

In the metaphorical dramas we refer to as "our lives," a series of dramatic personae is ever arriving at the doorways of our perception. What appears to the untrained eye as "life" is actually a screen of infinite pixels upon which we view the latest draft of our autobiography.

Whatever you refer to as "other" or as "the world out there," are really aspects of yourself you have abrogated, withdrawn from, and with which you must ultimately reconcile.

Jesus and Magdalena

Gazing at the stars, the fourteen-year-old Samarian beauty Magdalena, adorned with bracelets and earrings, body paint, glitter, toe rings, necklaces, and ankle bells, lay still with her head upon her scarf on the desert sand. Fifteen-year-old Yeshu ben Yoseif too looked up at the celestial lights with his head upon her lap, and spoke.

"There can never be true peace among our people. The Romans keep the peace for now, but we shall be opposed till the end of time, when Moshiach comes to restore the kingdom of Truth."

"But if you and I were to beget offspring, then our people could become one."

"It would never do for me to marry a girl who worships other gods, idols, graven images," he teased.

"I know there is one God. The statues are nothing but reminders. I do not bow to a golden calf like your ancestors. The images of the natural world are my people's testimony to the great works of the Mighty One."

"You are rare amongst the Samarians. I doubt your family has such insight, or that mine would accept such a fine line of philosophy."

"Yes I suppose."

"When Moshe looked across the Jordan into this land, it was revealed to him the entire future of the people of Israel. It is written of your people…"

"I know, in the Book of Numbers, that we'll be as thorns in your eyes, and as pricks in your sides, and harass you in the land wherein ye dwell."

"Yes, as your body has been harassing me since we first met. But your people will come to worship our God, the Living One, and be our enemies, murdering Jews and calling us the idol worshippers."

"But why would they, if they acknowledge the Hebrew God?"

"Because my people will become idolaters, not with golden calves, but false gods far more terrible and exceedingly clever: the god of wealth, the god of fame and power, the god of sensual pleasure, and the god of comfort and security. And the voices and images of these false gods will speak to us great lies upon terrible altars in every room of every dwelling. From blasphemous boxes, they will deliver unto our children an unholy, ungodly world.

"We will build great high places, much higher than the heathen altars of the old kings, abominations unto God, towering to the sky in praise of the false gods of money, celebrity, pleasure, and comfort. And Ha-Shem will command your people to strike these down, causing great suffering. Thus was revealed the future unto Moshe."

Einstein, Newton, and the Fish Tank

The first law of the fish tank states that the food appears at four p.m. Whether you believe in a higher power or in the legend of the alleged human, you had nevertheless better choose which of these flakes you want, before they all disappear.

Out on the game board known as the world, Mr. Newton has written some rules of gravity and motion to remind us we'll be passing "Go" and coming around, and what goes up must come down. It's good to know how it works on that little game board, in case we wish to play there.

But there is another body of law that overlaps the world. It says that what you find there depends on what you look for. And Mr. Einstein takes us out of the fish tank and off the game board to the place where the metaphors have been waiting four thousand years.

Messiah

The Savior, the Christ, Moshiach, the Avatar, Metteya, Messiah, the ultimate human manifestation, he who comes to herald the end of time, the return to the One, he who comes to shed light upon the true and the false, the soul and the ego, to reveal the Good, that always has been, while the evil, which never was, slips from our consciousness: Is he a man, this one whom we await?

Or is he within each of us? Perhaps your highest, truest, most gracious and sublime identity, if you could be all that you could be, the real you, the soul undiluted, operating within the world without being deceived about lesser identity, never losing the connection to the One, is even now observing, experiencing, and measuring for the right moment to emerge.

Is there truly a final and factual ultimate Return? Or is this the myth that narrates the return occurring in every moment? Is there to be a literal coming of the Christ, an Age of Moshiach, to be accomplished simultaneously for us all by God? Or is this to be performed by each within his soul as the living Infinity manifests and returns, across the entire creation and in each minutest part?

Like an M. C. Escher Symmetry, is the endless coming and going part of the essential divine nature, with one soul's return to union with Brahman as the very defining of another's birth in the world? Might one subjectively experience a total universal At-One-Ment, a return of all souls, while others actually see life go on as usual? Or is there truly an End? And then what?

Jesus and Magdalena

What is it that troubles you? Never have I seen you so downcast. What terrible dreams becloud your spirit?

The blackest darkness has enveloped me. The reason for my existence is mocked and made trivial. All the work of my life turns to shit. This has been revealed to me. For every soul who comes to know the living God through my teaching of Torah, shall one thousand declare me to be a god and blaspheme in my name. Multitudes shall worship the Father, but by bowing down to statues of me!

To be worshipped as a god troubles you? But these multitudes, be they gentiles? Shall this be the way by which the whole earth comes to praise God the Father? These who bow down today before stones and trees, animal likenesses and the stars? You are a prophet of Israel. Through you, they shall convert from idolatry to the Hebrew God.

All manner of horrors shall be committed in my name. A great slaughter of Jews, again and again, all throughout the coming history. By such devious trickery, the very keepers of the Torah shall be murdered as punishment for not joining with those who worship me. And the godless Romans, who worship murder and the rape of children, shall become the great champions of this cult, making it their banner of brutality, protecting the most abominable acts with a flimsy veneer of sanctity.

The Romans? You say they will worship God. But how can they worship God and spit on the Torah. It doesn't make sense.

Yes, it makes no sense. But somehow a few words from my teachings of the Torah shall become their holy scripture. These words will be used to explain, justify, and make excuses for any act, any moral position, any side of any debate. It is the dawning of the Age of Bullshit. And yet, you are right. Somehow the world will come to worship the one God, and the tidbits of Torah they remember from me will light their way. And of course, the Jews shall always be there, for we are the keepers of the entire Torah, the mystical roadmap between all the realms.

Yeshu Ben Yoseph Ponders the Role of Moshiach

When Jesus and his comrade, Ari, would converse about the Torah, about God, exploring religious philosophy, challenging each other to reach the outer cosmos and the innermost soul, they would forget about eating and sleeping, and even find themselves transported to foreign countries, improbable cultures, and distantly past or future times, all on the wings of their sincere inquiries of the inmost Self. Here we find the lads at a Parisian cafe, sipping tea, engrossed in their exchange of ideas, oblivious to the comings and goings of the worldly throng around them. Jesus speaks.

Your penultimate soul, the highest, truest, holiest Self, inseparable from the almighty, infinite One, and yet walking this earth, is the Moshiach, the redeemer, the savior of all souls, awaited and joyously anticipated by the children of Israel.

In following the Law, both in spirit as well as by the letter, you or I or any of us, by the grace of the Father, can attain our real identity: a living son of God, dispensing goodness and performing miracles across the land, healing the sick, feeding the poor, raising the dead.

For the hardness of our lives, the very solidity of the material world, are but the illusions we've lived by since choosing the apple of good and evil. Living in the elevated version of the world, the Kingdom of God, the only true Reality, there is only good. And the Moshiach is he whose eyes are open to seeing only the real, only the good.

Ari answers, Yes, but I wouldn't suggest proclaiming myself the Messiah just yet, as the rabbis are liable to take it quite literally. Many of us might attain our true inner Self, sitting at tea on a spring afternoon, but there will always be Romans to kick your head in as a test of whether you have truly reached the heights.

Jesus continues:

As I quest for oneness with my Father, to walk the earth as He would have me walk, according to His commandments, in the footsteps of the holy ones who came before, is not this the very quest to attain my highest Self, the Self which is none other than my Father who sent me?

Is not then the holy life, the spiritual path, defined not only by glorious revelation and graceful communion to be savored at every turn, but by the attempt to become the Moshiach, the Christ, the very destination within us, awaiting each of us at the end of the long and winding road?

Should it not be the highest goal of every Jew, pervading his night-long studies and his every prayer, to become so thoroughly holy, so fearless of man's world, so immersed in Truth, in Torah, in Talmud, so at-one with God, that his every breath spreads the living Word, and his glance brings souls from darkness back to Light?

Is it not well taught and established in the Torah that this Moshiach indeed dwells within each of us, and in fact is the real me and the real you, so that I am He as you are He and you are me, and we are All, together? I proclaim my Oneness with the Father, and therefore your Oneness, the same Oneness, there is none other.

The Never-ending Bible

Scripture is continuous. The words of the prophets are written every day, as the Tao continues its seamless Torah. Even on the television, the voice of idolatry is converted to blessings and truth for those willing to hear.

Warnings and admonitions, the stories of those who have gone astray, tales of darkness, tales of light emerge from the banalities of our culture.

Visionaries walk among us, offering new metaphors for the timeless, and sages rise from the poorest quarters, to sing our oneness on the airwaves.

Not My Opinion

To any who would say this is just opinion, this book is not an opinion of the writer. The ideas are not the product of an analytical process, but rather a gift which the writer has the privilege of passing along to the intended recipients.

Was it an opinion of John Keats that "beauty is Truth, Truth beauty?" Was it an opinion of Leonard Cohen that "there is a crack in everything: that's how the light gets in?" Was it an opinion of Bob Dylan that "jewels and binoculars hang from the head of the mule?"

And these visions, not earned by any special merit, were nevertheless bestowed in the transcendent place where the One meets the Many, and are offered in gratitude.

Even my best friends, they don't know
That my job is turning lead into gold
Out on the highway, hear that engine moan
I'm still searching for the philosopher's stone.

Van Morrison

"I Choose, I Chose" c. 2004 Noah Hosburgh, lino-cut

BOOK FOUR:
THE ROSETTA

A PHILOSOPHERS' STONE OF INTEGRATIVE MEDITATIONS

We will sample each of the six major world religions along with latter-day prophets, to demonstrate that they are actually expressions of the same perennial truths. Are their metaphors different? Certainly. Is there a difference in what the metaphors are for? No. Does one of these faiths hold the highest truth, above the others? Any metaphor that allows even one person to have a transcendent experience of the One is equally true and holy.

When you've seen beyond yourself, then you may find peace of mind is waiting there. And the time will come when you see we're all one, and life flows on within you and without you. (George Harrison)

1. Source
One is the holiest number.

Judaic: Hear O Israel, the Lord our God, the Lord is One. (Deuteronomy 6:4)

Christian: I and the Father are One. (John 10:30)

Islamic: He is the living One; there is no God but Him. (Koran 40:65)

Hindu: God is pure and ever One, and ever one they are in God. (Bhagavad Gita 5:19)

Taoist: Tao existed prior to the beginning of time as the single deep and subtle Reality. (Tao Te Ching 21)

Buddhist: Objectively nothing exists outside the Unity of Mind. (Tibetan Book of the Dead)

How the faces of love have changed. I'm turning the pages and I have changed, oh but You, You remain ageless. (Stevie Nicks)

2. Existence
The many manifestations all derive from the One.

Judaic: In the beginning God created the Heaven and the Earth. (Genesis 1:1)

Christian: Turn from these vanities unto the living God, which made heaven and earth, and the sea and all things that are therein. (Acts 14:15)

Islamic: It was He who created the heavens and the earth in all truth. When He says, "Be", so shall it be. (Koran 6:73)

Hindu: I am the One source of all: the evolution of all comes from me. (Bhagavad Gita 10:8)

Taoist: The Tao is called the Great Mother: empty yet inexhaustible, it gives birth to infinite worlds. (Tao Te Ching 6)

Buddhist: If you can look into the visions, you can experience and recognize that they are composed of the same pure clear white light as everything else in the universe. (Tibetan Book of the Dead)

Don't let it bring you down, it's only castles burning. Find someone who's turning and you will come around. (Neil Young)

3. Conditions
The apparencies of the relative world have little bearing upon your actual condition.

Judaic: Man doth not live by bread only, but by everything that procedeth out of the mouth of the Lord. (Deuteronomy 8:3)

Christian: Blessed in spirit are the poor, for theirs is the kingdom of heaven. (Matthew 5:3)

Islamic: That which you have been given is but the fleeting comfort of this life. Better and more enduring is God's reward to those who believe and put their trust in him. (Koran 42:36)

Hindu: The man whom these cannot move, whose soul is one, beyond pleasure and pain, is worthy of life in eternity. (Bhagavad Gita 2:15)

Taoist: When he no longer thinks of the personal body as self, neither failure nor success can ail him. (Tao Te Ching 13)

Buddhist: It is not life and wealth and power that enslave us, but the clinging to life and wealth and power. (TOB 18)

Turn off your mind, relax, and float downstream, it is not dying. Lay down all thought, surrender to the Void, it is shining. (John Lennon and Paul McCartney)

4. Surrender
Communion with the One is neither loss nor sacrifice, for it abolishes fear.

Judaic: After the Lord your God shall ye walk, and Him shall ye fear, and His commandments shall ye keep, and unto His voice shall ye hearken, and Him shall ye serve, and unto Him shall ye cleave. (Deuteronomy 13:5)

Christian: Seek the Lord and find him, though he be not far from every one of us. For in him we live, and move, and have our being. (Acts 17:28)

Islamic: I am commanded to surrender myself to the Lord of the Universe. (Koran 40:66)

Hindu: When a man surrenders all desires that come to the heart, and by the grace of God finds the joy of God, then his soul has indeed found peace. (Bhagavad Gita 2:55)

Taoist: Oneness with Tao is freedom from harm, indescribable pleasure, eternal life. (Tao Te Ching 16)

Buddhist: The gift of dharma exceeds all gifts, the sweetness of dharma exceeds all sweetness, the delight in dharma exceeds all delights. (Dhammapada 354)

Life is a mystery. Everyone must stand alone. I hear You call my name,
and it feels like Home. (Madonna)

5. Return

The illusion of separation, even for a million years, is but the blink of an eye. What awaits is that which we never left.

Judaic: In the end of days thou wilt return to the Lord thy God, and hearken unto his voice, for the Lord thy God is a merciful God. (Deuteronomy 4:30)

Christian: I came forth from the Father, and am come into the world: again, I leave the world, and go to the Father. (John 16:28)

Islamic: Surely to God all things shall in the end return. (Koran 42:53)

Hindu: Whatever path men travel is my path. No matter where they walk, it leads to me. (Bhagavad Gita 9:7)

Taoist: Tao sends forth a succession of living things as mysterious as the unbegotten existence to which they return. (Tao Te Ching 14)

Buddhist: Remember the pure, clear, white light from which everything in the universe comes, to which everything in the universe returns, the original nature of your own mind. (Tibetan Book of the Dead)

I don't claim to be guilty, but I do understand, there's a Law, there's an Arm, there's a Hand. (Leonard Cohen)

6. Punishment
The subjective experience of separation, in an increasingly physical way, is the inevitable consequence of acts performed in disregard of the One.

Judaic: I will forsake them and I will hide my face from them, and they shall be devoured, and many evils and troubles shall come upon them. (Deuteronomy 31:17)

Christian: What shall it profit a man if he shall gain the whole world and lose his own soul.(Mark 8:36)

Islamic: Just as Our revelations were declared to you and you forgot them, so on this day you are yourself forgotten. (Koran 20:126)

Hindu: Led astray by many wrong thoughts, entangled in the net of delusion, enchained to the pleasures of their cravings, they fall down into a foul hell. (Bhagavad Gita 16:16)

Taoist: The earth is like a vessel so sacred that at the mere approach of the profane it is marred, and when they reach out their fingers it is gone. (Tao Te Ching 29)

Buddhist: The fool thinks that the mischief he makes is as sweet as honey till it bears its fruit, and then he suffers. (Dhammapada 69)

I've a reason to believe we all will be received in Grace Land. (Paul Simon)

7. Reward
Your birthright of inner peace and immortality are regained by living in mindfulness of the One.

Judaic: Ye shall walk in all the way that the Lord your God commanded you, that ye may live, and that it may be well with you, and that ye may prolong your days in the land which ye shall possess. (Deuteronomy 5:30)

Christian: Being made free from sin, and become servants to God, ye have your fruit unto holiness, and the end everlasting life. For the wages of sin is death, but the gift of God is eternal life. (Romans 6:22)

Islamic: Whoever seeks the harvest of the world to come, to him We will give in great abundance. (Koran 42:20)

Hindu: When work is done for a reward, the work brings pleasure or pain or both, in its time; but when a man does work in eternity, then eternity is his reward. (Bhagavad Gita 18:12)

Taoist: Stay centered in the Tao and the world comes to you without harm, and finds contentment. (Tao Te Ching 35)

Buddhist: Those who hear this truth even once and listen with a grateful heart, treasuring it, revering it, gain blessings without end. (TTB 200)

If I seem to act unkind, it's only me, it's not my Mind that is confusing things. (John Lennon and Paul McCartney)

8. Justice
The sins we perceive in others will easily disappear when we cease projecting them from within ourselves.

Judaic: Create in me a clean heart, O God, and renew a right spirit within me. Then will I teach transgressors thy ways, and sinners shall be converted unto thee. (Psalms 51:9)

Christian: First cast out the beam out of thine own eye, and then shalt thou see clearly to cast out the mote out of thy brother's eye. (Matthew 7:5)

Islamic: Would you enjoin righteousness on others and forget it yourselves? (Koran 2:44)

Hindu: When he has no lust, no hatred, a man walks safely among the things of lust and hatred. (Bhagavad Gita 2:64)

Taoist: A good man, before he can help a bad man, finds in himself the matter with the bad man. (Tao Te Ching 27)

Buddhist: One should pay no heed to the faults of others, what they have done and not done. Rather should one consider the things oneself has done and not done. (Dhammapada 50)

Lord my body has been a good friend, but I won't need it when I reach the end. (Cat Stevens)

9. Death
The only death is upon a two-dimensional game-board in which a tiny part of you craves drama.

Judaic: Though I walk through the valley of the shadow of death I will fear no evil, for Thou art with me. (Psalms 23)

Christian: Fear not them which kill the body, but are not able to kill the soul. (Matthew 10:28)

Islamic: He sends forth guardians who watch over you and carry away your souls without fail when death overtakes you. Then are all men restored to God, their true Lord. (Koran 6:62)

Hindu: The wise grieve not for those who live and they grieve not for those who die, for life and death shall pass away. Because we all have been for all time: I and thou and those kings of men. And we shall be for all time, we all for ever and ever. (Bhagavad Gita 2:11)

Taoist: If you stay in the center and embrace death with your whole heart, you will endure forever. (Tao Te Ching 33)

Buddhist: Worldlings will regard as death what the conqueror of self knows to be life everlasting. (TOB 12:4)

Some people say the sky is just the sky, but I say, Why deny the obvious, child? Why deny the obvious? (Paul Simon)

10. Truth
There is nothing else but the One, and it is to be sought and found in all of the Many.

Judaic: He is the Rock, his work is perfect, for all his ways are justice: a God of truth. (Deuteronomy 32:4)

Christian: Seek ye first the Kingdom of Heaven, because that is where the laws of God operate truly, and they can operate only truly because they are the laws of truth. But seek this only, because you can find nothing else. There is nothing else. (A Course In Miracles 7:IV:7:1)

Islamic: God is Truth, and falsehood all that they invoke besides Him. (Koran 22:62)

Hindu: That which is non-existent can never come into being, and that which is can never cease to be. Those who have known the inmost reality know also the nature of is and is not. (Bhagavad Gita 2:16)

Taoist: One who is anciently aware of existence is master of every moment, feels no break since time beyond time in the way life flows. (Tao Te Ching 14)

Buddhist: Truth is perfect and complete in itself. It is not something newly discovered, it has always existed. Truth is not far away, it is ever present. It is not something to be attained, since not one of your steps leads away from it. (TTB 150)

I rode a tank, held a general's rank, when the blitzkrieg raged and the bodies stank. Pleased to meet you, hope you guess my name. But what's puzzling you is the nature of my game. (Mick Jagger and Keith Richards)

11. War
It is the metaphor of the struggle to prevail over all the ego's unworthy inclinations.

Judaic: And when the Lord thy God shall deliver them before thee, thou shalt smite them and utterly destroy them; thou shalt make no covenant with them, nor show mercy unto them. (Deuteronomy 7:2)

Christian: Think not that I am come to send peace on earth: I came not to send peace, but a sword. (Matthew 10:34)

Islamic: Slay them wherever you find them. Drive them out of the places from which they drove you. (Koran 2:191)

Hindu: There is no greater good for a warrior than to fight in a righteous war. There is a war that opens the doors of heaven. Happy the warriors whose fate is to fight such a war. (Bhagavad Gita 2:31)

Taoist: Men who have to fight for their living and are not afraid to die for it are higher men than those who, stationed high, are too fat to dare to die. (Tao Te Ching 75)

Buddhist: Though one man conquer a thousand men in battle a thousand times, he who conquers himself is the greatest warrior. (Dhammapada 103)

Soon you'll attain the stability you strive for in the only way that it's granted. (Paul Kantner)

12. Purpose
A decision to recognize the One must guide all our actions.

Judaic: Ye will seek the Lord thy God and thou shalt find Him if thou search after Him with all thy heart and with all thy soul. (Deuteronomy 4:29)

Christian: Who, when he came, and had seen the grace of God, was glad, and exhorted them all, that with purpose of heart they would cleave unto the Lord. (Acts 11:23)

Islamic: Those who dwell with God give glory to him night and day and are never wearied. (Koran 41:38)

Hindu: If your mind and heart are set upon me constantly, you will come to me. (Bhagavad Gita 8:7)

Taoist: To approach the Tao, you will need all your sincerity, for it is elusive, first revealing itself in form and image, then dissolving into subtle, indefinable essence. (Hua Hu Ching 68)

Buddhist: Mindfulness is the way to immortality, unmindfulness the way to death. Those who are mindful do not die, but the unmindful are already like the dead. (Dhammapada 21)

Human gods aim for their mark, made everything from toy guns that spark to flesh colored Christs that glow in the dark. (Bob Dylan)

13. Hypocrisy
These teachings are not intended for gain of status in the relative world, but rather for transcendence of the world and communion with the One.

Judaic: He flattereth himself in his own eyes, the words of his mouth are iniquity and deceit. He hath left off being wise and doing good. (Psalms 36:3)

Christian: Not every one that saith unto me Lord, Lord shall enter into the kingdom of heaven, but he that doeth the will of my father in heaven. (Matthew 7:21)

Islamic: Believers you are not. Rather say "We profess Islam", for faith has not yet found its way into your hearts. (Koran 49:14)

Hindu: Those who lack discrimination may quote the letter of the scripture, but they are really denying its inner truth. (Bhagavad Gita 2:42)

Taoist: False teachers of life use flowery words and start nonsense. The man of stamina stays with the root below the tapering, stays with the fruit beyond the flowering. (Tao Te Ching 38)

Buddhist: The essentials of the holy life do not consist in the profits of gain, honor, and a good name, nor even in the profits of observing moral rules, nor even in the profits of insight, but the sure heart's release. (TTB 64)

*For each unharmful, gentle soul misplaced inside a jail, we gazed upon
the Chimes of Freedom flashing. (Bob Dylan)*

14. Forgiveness
Off-stage we shall warmly thank our friends and enemies alike, for their indispensable roles in our journey.

Judaic: The Lord is slow to anger and plenteous in loving kindness, forgiving iniquity and transgression. (Numbers 14:18)

Christian: If ye forgive men their trespasses, your heavenly Father will also forgive you. (Matthew 6:14)

Islamic: Requite evil with good, and he who is your enemy will become your dearest friend. (Koran 41:34)

Hindu: Though a man be soiled with the sins of a lifetime, let him but love me, rightly resolved, and in utter devotion: I see no sinner. That man is holy. (Bhagavad Gita 9:30)

Taoist: I am kind to the kind. I am also kind to the unkind. Thus kindness is attained. (Tao Te Ching 49)

Buddhist: If someone foolishly does me wrong, I will return to that person the protection of my ungrudging love. (TOB 33:2)

We are stardust, we are golden, caught in the devil's bargain, and we've got to get ourselves back to the Garden. (Joni Mitchell)

15. Faith
Even in the darkness of the ego's world, remembering our true nature brings meaning and light.

Judaic: Our soul waiteth for the Lord. He is our help and our shield. For our heart shall rejoice in him, because we have trusted in his holy name. (Psalms 33:20)

Christian: I am the resurrection and the life. He that believeth in me, though he were dead, yet shall he live. And whosoever believeth in me shall never die. (John 11:25)

Islamic: Yes, by the lord, you shall assuredly be raised to life. (Koran 64:7)

Hindu: For this is my word of promise, that he who loves me shall not perish. (Bhagavad Gita 9:31)

Taoist: If the people of the world were wise enough to plant the root of their lives deep within the Subtle Origin, then the worldly affairs of life would coherently follow their own natural course, and harmony would abound of its own accord. (Tao Te Ching 37)

Buddhist: Wide open is the door of immortality to all who have ears to hear. May they receive the Dharma with faith. (TOB 12:13)

I choose the rooms that I live in with care, the windows are small and the walls almost bare, there's only one bed and only one prayer, I listen all night for your step on the stair. (Leonard Cohen)

<u>16. Humility</u>
We regain our communion with the One by minimizing our separate egos.

Judaic: The meek shall inherit the earth, and shall delight themselves in the abundance of peace. (Psalms 37:11)

Christian: Whosoever of you will be the chiefest, shall be servant of all. (Mark 10:44)

Islamic: Do not walk proudly on the earth. You cannot cleave the earth, nor can you rival the mountains in stature. (Koran 17:37)

Hindu: The man who forsakes all desires and abandons all pride of possession and of self reaches the goal of peace supreme. (Bhagavad Gita 2:71)

Taoist: High beings of deep universal virtue work unassertively. They help all people, yet people are barely aware of their existence. (Tao Te Ching 17)

Buddhist: He who does not cling to his name and his status and who possesses nothing will not be destroyed by his sorrow. (Dhammapada 221)

I am He as you are He as you are me and we are All, together. (John Lennon and Paul McCartney)

17. God In Man
To see each living thing as a manifestation of the One is to awaken awareness of the One within you.

Judaic: And God created man in His own image, in the image of God created He him; male and female created He them. (Genesis 1:27)

Christian: I am the way, the truth, and the life: no man cometh unto the Father but by me. (John 14:6)

Islamic: He molded him and breathed into him of His spirit. (Koran 32:8)

Hindu: And when he sees me in all, and he sees all in me, then I never leave him and he never leaves me. (Bhagavad Gita 6:30)

Taoist: Because he does not hold a narrow concept of self, his true nature can fully merge with the one universal life. (Tao Te Ching 7)

Buddhist: Your own conscious awareness, unceasing, bright, distinct, and vibrant, just this awareness is the Father, Buddha, all-around goodness. (Tibetan Book of the Dead)

Wild child full of grace, savior of the human race, your cool face, natural child, terrible child, not your mother's or your father's child, you're our child, screaming, wild. (Jim Morrison)

18. Child
Wisdom and guidance are offered to you in the simplicity and innocence of the baby and your own child-nature.

Judaic: For unto us a child is born, unto us a son is given, and the government shall be upon his shoulder. And his name shall be called Wonderful, Counselor, the mighty God, the everlasting Father, the Prince of Peace. (Isaiah 9:6)

Christian: Except ye be converted, and become as little children, ye shall not enter into the kingdom of heaven. (Matthew 18:3)

Islamic: How can we speak with a babe in the cradle? Whereupon he spoke and said, "I am the servant of God. He has given me the Book and ordained me a prophet." (Koran 19:29)

Hindu: When born he reached beyond the earth, behind and also before. (Rigveda 10:90:5)

Taoist: Never departing from the eternal power of Tao, you become as an infant once again, immortal. (Tao Te Ching 28)

Buddhist: You must neither enjoy the visions nor fear them, and thus neither think they are important nor cling to them: this is what we call keeping your mind as if it were a child. (TTB 171)

Mine is the sunlight, mine is the morning, born of the One Light, Eden saw play. Praise with elation, praise every morning God's re-creation of the new day. (Cat Stevens)

<u>19. Owns All</u>
Only as an excellent guest in the visible world can we hope to reveal the pristine garden waiting behind the curtain.

Judaic: Behold, unto the Lord thy God belongeth the heaven, and the heaven of heavens, the earth with all that therein is. (Deuteronomy 10:14)

Christian: Of Him and through Him, and to Him are all things, to whom be glory forever. (Romans 11:36)

Islamic: To God belongs all that the heavens and the earth contain. (Koran 4:131)

Hindu: He contains all works and desires and all perfumes and all tastes. He enfolds the whole universe, and in silence is loving to all. (Chandogya Upanishad)

Taoist: The great Tao floods and flows in every direction. Everything in existence depends on it, and it doesn't deny them. (Tao Te Ching 34)

Buddhist: This pure Mind, the source of everything, shines forever and on all with the brilliance of its own perfection. (TTB 194)

I may not have a lot to give, but what I've got I'll give to you. I don't care too much for money, money can't buy me love. (John Lennon and Paul McCartney)

20. Wealth
True riches can be recognized even amongst the glitter of superficial distractions.

Judaic: Wisdom is better than rubies, and all the things that may be desired are not to be compared to it. (Proverbs 8:11)

Christian: Lay up for yourselves treasure in heaven, where neither moth nor rust doth corrupt, and where thieves do not break through nor steal, for where your treasure is, there will your heart be also. (Matthew 6:20)

Islamic: Do not regard with envy the worldly benefits We have bestowed on some among them, for with these We seek only to try them. Better is your Lord's reward, and more lasting. (Koran 20:131)

Hindu: I know that treasures pass away and that the eternal is not reached by the transient. (Katha Upanishad 2:10)

Taoist: One of deep virtue is not occupied with amassing material goods, yet the more he lives for others, the richer his life becomes. (Tao Te Ching 81)

Buddhist: I cannot give him perishable treasures that will bring cares and sorrows, but I can give him the inheritance of a holy life, which is a treasure that will not perish. (TOB 22:11)

As good as you've been to this world, so good I'm going to be right back to you. (Janis Joplin)

21. Golden Rule
We inevitably treat others according to how much we recognize the One and the Many in ourselves.

Judaic: Thou shalt love thy neighbor as thyself. (Leviticus 19:18)

Christian: All things whatsoever ye would that men should do to you, do ye even so to them. (Matthew 7:12)

Islamic: Give just measure and defraud none. Weigh with even scales and do not cheat your fellow men of what is rightly theirs. (Koran 26:183)

Hindu: And when a man sees that the God in himself is the same God in all that is, he hurts not himself by hurting others. (Bhagavad Gita 13:28)

Taoist: To the highly evolved being, there is no such thing as tolerance, because there is no such thing as other. She has given up all ideas of individuality and extended her goodwill without prejudice in every direction. (Hua Hu Ching 15)

Buddhist: Since each and every person is so precious to themselves, the self-respecting harm no other being. (TTB 121)

Lord, kiss me once more, fill me with song. Allah, kiss me once more, that I
may wear my love like heaven. (Donovan)

<u>22. Prayer</u>
The Source of all is accessible within you.

Judaic: Come! Let us sing to Ha-Shem, let us call out to the Rock of our salvation. Let us greet Him with thanksgiving, with praiseful songs let us call out to Him. (Psalms 95:1)

Christian: Pray one for another, that ye may be healed. The effectual fervent prayer of a righteous man availeth much. (James 5:16)

Islamic: Proclaim the portions of the Book that are revealed to you and be steadfast in prayer. Prayer fends away indecency and evil, but your foremost duty is to remember God. (Koran 29:45)

Hindu: He who filled with devotion recites this supreme mystery, prepares in truth for Eternity. (Katha Upanishad 3:17)

Taoist: When people of the highest awareness hear the subtle Way of the universe, they cultivate themselves diligently in order to live in accord with it. (Tao Te Ching 41)

Buddhist: In the palace of bright, pure wisdom's universal bliss, with reverent devotion, ardently I pray. (Tibetan Book of the Dead)

There's nothing you can know that isn't known, nothing you can see that isn't shown, nowhere you can be that isn't where you're meant to be. (John Lennon and Paul McCartney)

23. Knows All
In One-ness there are no secrets.

Judaic: The eyes of the Lord are in every place, beholding the evil and the good. (Proverbs 15:3)

Christian: I know thy works, and tribulation, and poverty. But thou art rich. (Revelations 2:9)

Islamic: He has knowledge of all that goes into the earth and all that springs up from it; all that comes down from heaven and all that ascends to it. (Koran 34:2)

Hindu: I know all that was and is and is to come, but no one in truth knows me. (Bhagavad Gita 7:26)

Taoist: When life is ruled by undisturbable Simplicity, desire and passion naturally fall away and reveal people's true, original nature. (Tao Te Ching 37)

Buddhist: Knowing the requirements of every single being, He does not reveal Himself to all alike. He does not impart to them at once the fullness of omniscience, but pays attention to the disposition of various beings. (TOB 32:11)

I'll tell it and think it and speak it and breathe it, and reflect it from the mountain so all souls can see it. (Bob Dylan)

24. Shine Your Light
Bring salvation to others and yourself by forwarding and demonstrating these teachings.

Judaic: Make me to understand the way of thy precepts: so shall I talk of thy wondrous works. (Psalms 119:27)

Christian: Go ye therefore and teach all nations, baptizing them in the name of the Father, the Son, and the Holy Spirit, teaching them to observe all things whatsoever I have commanded you. (Matthew 28:19)

Islamic: Say, "It is God who gives you life and later causes you to die. It is He who will gather you all on the Day of Resurrection." (Koran 45:26)

Hindu: The wise who can learn and can teach this ancient story find glory in the world of Brahman. (Katha Upanishad 3:16)

Taoist: If you wish to gain merit and become one with the divine, then develop your virtue and extend it to the world. (Hua Hu Ching 72)

Buddhist: There are some beings that are almost free from the dust of worldliness. If they hear not the doctrine preached, they will be lost. But if they hear it, they will believe and be saved. (TOB 12:11)

The fishes will laugh as they swim out of the path, and the seagulls they'll be smiling. And the rocks on the sand will proudly stand, the hour that the ship comes in. (Bob Dylan)

<u>25. Savior</u>
We await the day when out of the Many shall emerge a personification of the truth and majesty of the One. This event is available in every moment.

Judaic: They shall cry unto the Lord because of the oppressors, and He shall send them a savior, and a great one, and he shall deliver them. (Isaiah 19:20)

Christian: Unto them that look for him shall he appear the second time without sin unto salvation. (Hebrews 9:28)

Islamic: You are one of Our messengers. Of these messengers We have exalted some above others. To some God spoke directly; others He raised to a lofty status. (Koran 2:252)

Hindu: In every age I come back to deliver the holy, to destroy the sin of the sinner, to establish righteousness. (Bhagavad Gita 4:7)

Taoist: The sage embraces the Oneness of the Tao, and becomes a guide for the whole world. (Tao Te Ching 22)

Buddhist: In due time another Buddha will arise in the world, a holy one, a supremely enlightened one, endowed with wisdom in conduct, auspicious, knowing the universe, an incomparable leader of men, a master of angels and mortals. He will reveal to you the same eternal truths which I have taught you. (TOB 43:13)

I'm standing at the crossroads, trying to read the signs, to tell me which way I should go to find the answer. And all the time I know: Plant your love and let it grow. (Eric Clapton)

26. Guidance
Open to the One, we naturally act rightly in the world.

Judaic: The Lord is my shepherd, I shall not want. He maketh me to lie down in green pastures, he leadeth me beside the still waters. He restoreth my soul. (Psalms 23:1)

Christian: Take no thought beforehand what ye shall speak, neither do ye premeditate. But whatsoever shall be given you in that hour, that speak ye, for it is not ye that speak, but the Holy Spirit. (Mark 13:11)

Islamic: Those that accept My guidance shall have nothing to fear or to regret. (Koran 2:38)

Hindu: God gives wisdom to the simple, and leadeth the wise unto the path of good. (Rig Veda 7:86:7)

Taoist: He cherishes what is deep within rather than what is shallow without. Knowing this, he knows what to accept and what to reject. (Tao Te Ching 39)

Buddhist: Faithful is one who is possessed of knowledge, seeing the way that leads to Nirvana; one who is not a partisan; one who is pure and virtuous, and has removed the veil from the eyes. Such a one will wander rightly in the world. (TOB 35:7)

When I look out my window, what do you think I see? And when I look inside my window, so many different people to be. (Donovan)

27. Constellation
We select and connect a million points of light to compose our unique individual journey.

Judaic: For as he thinketh in his heart, so is he. (Proverbs 23:7)

Christian: And Heaven itself but represents your will, where everything created is for you. No spark of life but was created with your glad consent, as you would have it be. And not one Thought that God has ever had but waited for your blessing to be born. (A Course In Miracles 30:II:1:8)

Islamic: God does not change a people's lot unless they change what is in their hearts. (Koran 13:11)

Hindu: This body is called the Field because a man sows seeds of action in it, and reaps their fruits. Wise men say that the Knower of the field is he who watches what takes place within this body. (Bhagavad Gita 13:1)

Taoist: Focus on Tao and you'll experience Tao. Focus on power and you'll experience power. Focus on loss and you'll experience loss. (Tao Te Ching 23)

Buddhist: All that we are is the result of what we have thought. It is founded on our thoughts, it is made up of our thoughts. (Dhammapada:1)

*You can't always get what you want, but if you try sometimes you'll find
you get what you need. (Mick Jagger and Keith Richards)*

<u>28. Gives All</u>
Everything required for our journey is provided.

Judaic: You open Your hand and satisfy the desire of every living thing.
(Psalms 145:16)

Christian: Your heavenly Father knoweth that ye have need of all these
things. But seek ye first the kingdom of God, and his righteousness; and all
these things shall be added unto you. (Matthew 7:32)

Islamic: It is He who sends down water from the sky with which We bring
forth every kind of plant, saying: "Eat and graze your cattle". (Koran
20:54)

Hindu: I shall supply all his needs, and protect his possessions from loss.
(Bhagavad Gita 9:22)

Taoist: Be content with what you have; rejoice in the way things are. When
you realize there is nothing lacking, the whole world belongs to you. (Tao
Te Ching 44)

Buddhist: How boundless and free is the sky of Awareness! How bright
the full moon of wisdom! Truly, is anything missing now? Nirvana is right
here before our eyes; this very place is the Lotus Land; this very body, the
Buddha. (TTB 200)

When I'm sad, She comes to me, with a thousand smiles She gives to me free. It's alright, She says it's alright, take anything you want from me, anything. (Jimi Hendrix)

29. Charity
By giving freely, as does the One to the Many with infinite generosity, we can rise to our true nature.

Judaic: He that giveth unto the poor shall not lack; but he that hideth his eyes shall have many a curse. (Proverbs 28:27)

Christian: And above all these things put on charity, which is the bond of perfectness. (Colossians 3:14)

Islamic: Whatever alms you give shall rebound to your own advantage, provided that you give them for the love of God. (Koran 2:272)

Hindu: A gift is pure when it is given from the heart to the right person at the right time and at the right place, and when we expect nothing in return. (Bhagavad Gita 17:20)

Taoist: To practice virtue is to selflessly offer assistance to others, giving without limitation one's time, abilities, and possessions in service, whenever and wherever needed, without prejudice concerning the identity of those in need. If your willingness to give blessings is limited, so also is your ability to receive them. (Hua Hu Ching 4)

Buddhist: The miser can never enter heaven and the fool scorns generosity. But the wise man finds joy in giving and enters heaven in this world. (Dhammapada 177)

Each of us has his own special gift, and you know this was meant to be true. (Bob Dylan)

30. Know Thyself
Only upon accepting our actual state can we find our unique route to our higher self.

Judaic: Lord, make me to know mine end, and the measure of my days, what it is, that I may know how frail I am. (Psalms 39:4)

Christian: For I say, through the grace given unto me, to every man that is among you, not to think of himself more highly than he ought to think; but to think soberly, according as God hath dealt to every man the measure of faith. (Romans 12:3)

Islamic: He has given you the earth for your heritage and exalted some of you in rank above others, so that He might prove you with His gifts. (Koran 6:165)

Hindu: And do thy duty, even if it be humble, rather than another's, even if it be great. To die in one's duty is life, to live in another's is death. (Bhagavad Gita 3:35)

Taoist: Completely emancipated from his former false life, he discovers his original pure nature, which is the pure nature of the universe. (Hua Hu Ching 77)

Buddhist: Your work is to find out what your work should be, and not to neglect it for another's. Clearly discover your work and attend to it with all your heart. (Dhammapada 166)

Meditation

Meditation, a form of prayer, is an activity performed for the purpose of transcendence. To transcend is "to pass beyond human limit, and exist above and independent of material experience." (American Heritage Dictionary)

Choose a time and location free of distractions and work-a-day demands. Sit in a **comfortable** position, whether cross-legged on the floor, or on a chair with feet flat on the floor, hands on lap or knees. Observe your body position head to toe to ensure you are as free of physical stress as possible.

With eyes lightly closed, breathe in slowly through the nose, without raising your chest or shoulders, by expanding your abdomen outward. Breathe out slowly through the nose by allowing your abdomen to return inward. Use two to three complete breath cycles per minute.

Mantra: For the entire duration of inhaling, think the sound "ah" (aaaaaaaaahhhhhhh). For the entire duration of exhaling, think the sound "ying." (yiiiiiiiiiiiiinnnnngg). Rather than doing anything with your mouth or vocal apparatus, permit the sounds to fill your inner space.

Continue regardless of any thoughts that come and go. If you notice you've gotten distracted by a chain of thought, just return to the mantra. Even if you were distracted for several minutes, this is okay. Noticing that this has occurred, and returning to the mantra, is a key part of the meditation.

Try to do this daily, at a similar time and place each day, for at least fifteen minutes. You should begin to notice, during the meditation, that the material world and all its cares occupy a smaller part of your totality. You may sense your personal space extending beyond the borders of the body, as you continue to simply "be here now." This is transcendence, and it has no limitations, since you are infinite.

After entering transcendence you can use the integrative meditations outlined earlier in this chapter by contemplating any section. See how the quotations, if not synonymous, are pointing towards the same essential truth, much like six coin-operated binoculars on the rim of the Grand Canyon.

Meditations on Oneness

Part One:

Do this meditation after reaching transcendence. Think the first section of each line while breathing in, and the "are One" while breathing out. It is an expansion of the words of Rabbi Yeshu Ben Yoseif, from John 10:30, into six synonymous declarations of the same truth.

I and the Father are One.	I and the Tao are One.
I and Brahman are One.	I and Ha-Shem are One.
I and Allah are One.	I and God are One.

Part Two:

This is best done outdoors, in a space of natural beauty such as a beach or park. It is done with eyes open. Extend your attention to include a gradually greater space. Start with your body, then include all of the surroundings, the big round planet beneath you, the sky below and above, and the entire celestial sphere. No need to turn your head, but just extend attention infinitely outward in all directions, while meditating "**I**" (the personal pronoun). This takes only about twenty or thirty seconds per sitting, and is intended to correct our misidentification of ourselves as small, limited beings.

Metaphorical Meditation

"God" is a word for that which cannot be put into words.

"Ha-Shem" is a word for that which cannot be put into words.

"Allah" is a word for that which cannot be put into words.

"Brahman" is a word for that which cannot be put into words.

"Tao" is a word for that which cannot be put into words.

"That-which-cannot-be-put-into-words" is a word for that which cannot be put into words.

Meditation on the Rosetta Precepts

The One is always and forever
    Becoming the Many

The Many are always and forever
    Becoming the One

The entire One is accessible
    In each of the Many

The One is alive
    And is the only aliveness there is

The One is conscious
    And is the only consciousness there is

There is nothing else
    But the One

"Monks Listening to Water" c. 2004 Noah Hosburgh, palm tree fibers and black plastic

There Is But One Religion

Each teaching has been adapted with a different name of God from the customary translations, but the meanings are entirely unchanged. None of these lines has been altered. The One has been referred to by many names and is still the One.

Judaic: HEAR OH ISRAEL, THE TAO.
OUR GOD, THE TAO, IS ONE.

Christian: OUR BRAHMAN WHICH ART IN HEAVEN
HALLOWED BE THY NAME.

Islamic: LA ILLAHA ILLA ENDLESS MIND.
("There is no god other than the Endless Mind.")

Hindu: HAR-E ALLAH, HAR-E ALLAH
ALLAH ALLAH, HAR-E HAR-E.
("Praise God.")

Taoist: THE GOD WHICH CAN BE DESCRIBED IN WORDS
IS NOT THE TRUE ETERNAL GOD.

Buddhist: HA-SHEM IS OUTSIDE OF STABILITY AND
OUTSIDE OF CHANGE, NEVER ORIGINATING
AND NEVER PASSING AWAY.

BOOK FIVE: IDOLS

Dharma Versus Dogma In Religion and Science

If it is true that "objectively nothing exists outside the Unity of Mind," then science, in all its branches, is but metaphor. If the Tao is "the single deep and subtle reality of the universe," then everything but the One is subjective. Rather than a definitive description of the workings of the world, the laws of science comprise a rulebook we regularly revise, a continuing catalog of constellation.

Einstein's offering in 1905 of a Theory of Relativity opened an era of scientific discoveries that began to approximate the precepts chanted by prehistoric people, later written down in China, India, and Israel as the world's holy books. As new breakthroughs in particle physics, virtual reality, and information theory proceed towards the ultimate Theory of Everything, the hallowed halls of objectivity have conceded mounting evidence that what we call "life" and "the world" are subjective: what is viewed depends upon the state of the viewer.

The implications are that each of us wields amazing power in our postulation of existence, as the potential architects of a golden age. But instead of a new universal entity, we seem to prefer the chain of folly, as science is seen as a source of games and gadgets, weapons and wonder drugs, for a faster rendition of the lamentable human chronicle.

Similarly, the teachings of every religion offer stability and certainty upon the only solid ground there is, as well as a state of mind in which we can peek through the curtains concealing our role in creation. But every such principle can turn into the fixed idea that does all our thinking for us. The very faith that set you free becomes an authoritarian mind control device when you slip from metaphorical to literal thinking.

What Is Meant By "Idolatry?"

It is not science and religion that manufacture false idols. In our urgency to have a world that won't go away, we make monuments of the metaphors and the myths that once brought light, and we bow down before them. Each faith admonishes us not to go looking for Love in all the wrong places.

Judaic: Thou shalt have no other gods before me. Thou shalt not make unto thee a graven image, even any likeness of any thing that is in heaven above, the earth below, or the water under the earth: thou shalt not bow down unto them nor serve them. (Deut. 5:7)

Christian: Idols are limits. They are the belief that there are forms that will bring happiness, and that, by limiting, is all attained. It is as if you said, "I have no need of everything. This little thing I want, and it will be everything to me." (A Course In Miracles 30:III:1:4)

Islamic: They worship helpless idols, which can confer on them no benefits from heaven or earth. Compare none with God. (Koran 16:73)

Hindu: If one selfishly sees a thing as if it were everything, independent of the One and the Many, then one is in the darkness of ignorance. (Bhagavad Gita 18:22)

Taoist: The Tao gives rise to all forms, yet it has no form of its own. If you attempt to fix a picture of it in your mind, you will lose it. This is like pinning a butterfly: the husk is captured, but the flying is lost. (Hua Hu Ching 6)

Buddhist: Look at this glittering world: it is like a royal carriage. The foolish are taken up by it, but the wise do not cling to it. (Dhammapada 171)

When we practice the form of a religion without regard to its inner meaning, or use its teachings to justify harming others, we engage in idolatry. When we fantasize that our pain or misfortune, or our pleasure and happiness, are from a source outside ourselves, that too is idol worship. In anger, fear, or any negative emotions, we are bowing down to empty forms we've empowered over us. Any moment spent in a world that is fixed and solid, as if beyond the influence of the wand we wave, is idolatry.

The Metaphors of September 11

On Saturday morning, September 8, 2001, Julius Cohen stepped to the *bimah* after Rabbi Zweig called him by his Hebrew name, and gestured to approach the Torah for the first *aliyah*. *Blessed art thou, oh Lord, our God, king of the universe, who selected us from all the peoples and gave us His Torah.* Mr. Cohen's presence on *Shabbos* was irregular, but he remembered enough from his pre-*bar Mitzvah* days to sing the blessing of the Torah in adequate Hebrew, reading the transliterated words from the card.

Rabbi Abraham Zweig, the spiritual leader of the Chabad Jewish Community Center of a small New England city, began the reading of the week's Torah portion, *Ki Tavo (Deuteronomy 26:1-29:8)*, the same which was being chanted in every synagogue around the world that day. He sang the first of the seven sections in his resonant baritone.

Now the Rabbi turned around and spoke to his congregation. "The Alter Rebbe, the founder of *Chabad Hassidism*, two hundred years ago, said to his adherents that they must live with the times. What does this mean, 'live with the times'? What's he telling them? To be fashionable? To drive to the mall and buy bell-bottoms or get body piercing? Well, to live with the times means to live with the week's Torah portion. This is your Hebrew horoscope for the week. Astrology, tarot, numerology, all these things come from Torah and Kabala. Did you know that? Every week we read the *parsha,* and it tells us what we need to pay attention to, in our families and our jobs and the nations of the world. We live with it.

"So how do we live with the curses listed in this week's *parsha? 'The Lord will bring a nation against thee from afar, as the vulture swoopeth down, a nation whose tongue thou shalt not understand. And he shall besiege thee in all thy gates, until thy high and fenced walls come down.' (Deuteronomy 28:52)* What does this mean to us today? Are we supposed to get ready for war? Are we about to be bombed? The important message is that the 'high and fenced walls' of our egos are never secure. If we build in our mind a separate kingdom as if we can get along just fine without God, then sooner or later it must come down, to make room for us to let Ha-Shem back into our life.

"We've been looking to our house, or car, or our business, as the solid ground we stand on, and we're proud of these things, but then, God forbid, we should lose them: *'And thy life shall hang in doubt before thee, and thou shalt fear day and night, and shalt have none assurance of thy life.' (Deuteronomy 28:66)* There is no assurance outside of God. We should all have many wonderful things, but always know where they come from. Everything is from God. The higher we build walls to glorify our ego, the more we fear, and the harder we fall."

Meanwhile, Mohammed Atta knelt upon his rug in the apartment he would soon be vacating permanently. In his hands was the Koran, and it was open to a verse he didn't need to look at to recite verbatim. *Slay them wherever you find them. Drive them out of the places from which they drove you. (2:191)* He remembered his first teacher, from the religious school he attended in

86

Cairo as a boy. This sheikh, though revered at the time, seemed hopelessly weak today.

"The Koran is not a book of murder! That is not the way one prepares himself for the return to Allah! In this glorious book, God speaks in metaphors to men. 'The Jews' and 'the unbelievers' represent the enemy within us, the forces of temptation and compromise we must overcome. *Make war on them until idolatry shall cease and God's religion shall reign supreme. (8:39)* Our life struggle is to find and remove the idolaters from our own soul. That is *jihad*, not the killing of innocents of other faiths, God forbid!"

But on this day Mr. Atta, a young man of mindfulness, discipline, and intensity, schooled in a severe rendition of Islam, was an officer in a very literal holy war. Several printouts of flight schedules were laid out on his table, the blueprints of martyrdom or mass murder, depending upon the branch to which you belong.

On Monday morning, September 10, as on every Monday, a small section of the weekly portion is read from the Torah, to prepare early in the week to order one's thoughts and actions in accordance with God's words. Rabbi Zwieg sang the first section of *Nitzavin-Vayelech (Deuteronomy 29:9-31:32)*, as was being done in every synagogue throughout the world.

And all the nations will say, Why did the Lord do so to this land? What is the reason for this great rage of fury? Then they will say, It is because they abandoned the covenant of the Lord, God of their fathers, the covenant which He made with them when He took them out of the land of Egypt. For they went and served other deities, prostrating themselves to them, deities which they had not known, and which He had not apportioned to them. (Deuteronomy 29:23)

"The Torah gives us the opportunity to learn the hard way or the soft way. Of all the commandments, none of them get half as much attention as this, the injunction against idols, other gods. Why is that? Of millions of Jews in the world, how many are literally bowing down to statues? So, why so many warnings? Because idolatry is very, very subtle. In the diaspora, we're scattered amongst all the nations. And we're presented every day with idols of sex and money and power. If you're not living with Torah every day, then you'll be worshipping them one way or another."

That same morning, in a motel room in Scarborough, Maine, Mohammed Atta re-confirms American Flight 11 for tomorrow, Tuesday, September 11. Outwardly a pleasant young man, inwardly reciting, *We will put terror into the hearts of the unbelievers. They serve other deities besides God for whom He has revealed no sanction. The fire shall be their home; dismal indeed is the dwelling of the evil-doers. (Koran 3:150)*

As if hearing the voice of mercy standing upon his right shoulder, he recalled the teacher of his childhood, reciting from scripture, *Then your Lord declared that He would raise against them others who would oppress them cruelly till the Day of Resurrection...We dispersed them through the earth in multitudes—some were righteous men, others were not—and tested them with blessings and misfortunes so that they might return to the right path. (7:167)*

"It is God alone," clarified the sheikh, "who brings forth tests and decides who has gone astray. Some may be severely oppressed to try their faith, while others are tested with riches. For a man to pass judgment in these matters is a great blasphemy, pretending to be God."

But the young soldier was too far along his grim journey, and kept his focus on verses he could understand at face value. *Wherever you be, death will overtake you, though you put yourselves in lofty towers. (4:78)*

On September 11, the towers of the World Trade Center came down.

On Wednesday, September 12, invisible to the naked eye, Jesus, the prophet of the Gospels, and Mohammed, the prophet of the Koran, sat upon camels atop the rubble at ground zero.

Mohammed speaks, quoting from the Bible, *And this house which is high shall be an astonishment to everyone that passeth by it so that he shall say, Why hath the Lord done thus unto this land, and unto this house? (II Chronicles 7:21)*

Jesus replies, *And when the angel stretched out his hand upon Jerusalem to destroy it, the Lord repented him of the evil and said to the angel that destroyed the people, It is enough: stay now thine hand. (II Samuel 24:16)*

Mohammed quotes a verse from the Koran, *God is forgiving and merciful... they shall become your brothers in the Faith. (9:11)*

Hands joined, the two prophets, Muslim and Jew, proclaim their agreement concerning the history of Israel as the metaphor of mankind dwelling in the material world.

"But doesn't it give you the willies, such exquisitely rendered prophesy lost on those who live on a surface world with barely a sliver of their Self, needing to physically enact the scriptural curses?"

"Spooks me out. They have to learn everything the hard way. That's why it's called the Long and Winding Road. But who are we to question? We just point to the truth. A few turn and look, and the rest fight over the fingertip."

Ascending and Descending

She said go back, go back to the world. (Leonard Cohen)

We find in all the faiths a formula for complete immersion in the affairs of living: to not reject the world, but rather to sanctify it by mindfulness in our handling of every detail. From the hundreds of meticulously observed Hebrew commandments, to the Zen Buddhist 'chop wood, carry water,' it is to the physical world that we are directed, to discover God in the daily doingness of hands-on living, lest we float off into flimsiness and unreality.

Judaic: Commit thy works unto the Lord, and thy thoughts shall be established. (Proverbs 16:3)

Christian: The works that I do in my Father's name, they bear witness of me. (John 10:25)

Islamic: Blessed is the reward of those who labor patiently and put their trust in their lord. (Koran 29:59)

Hindu: Freedom from action is never achieved by abstaining from it...The world is imprisoned in its own activity, except when actions are performed as worship of God. Therefore you must perform every action sacramentally, and be free from all attachments to results. (Bhagavad Gita 3:9)

Taoist: Man at his best, like water, serves as he goes along. Like water he seeks his own level, the common level of life, loves living close to the earth, living clear down in his heart, loves kinship with his neighbors, the pick of words that tell the truth, the even tenor of a well-run state, the fair profit of able dealing, the right timing of useful deeds. (Tao Te Ching 8)

Buddhist: Rouse yourself and follow the enlightened way through the world with energy and joy. (Dhammapada 168)

BOOK SIX:
SONGS

Six Versions of a Prayer

Judaic:
The Lord is my shepherd; I shall not want
He maketh me to lie down in green pastures, he leadeth me beside the still waters
He restoreth my soul. He leadeth me in the paths of righteousness for his name's sake
Yea, though I walk through the valley of the shadow of death, I will fear no evil, for thou art with me. Thy rod and thy staff they comfort me.
Thou preparest a table before me in the presence of mine enemies. Thou annointest my head with oil, my cup runneth over.
Surely goodness and mercy shall follow me all the days of my life, and I will dwell in the house of the Lord forever. (Psalms 23)

Christian:
Our Father which art in heaven, hallowed be thy name.
Thy kingdom come. Thy will be done, in earth as it is in heaven.
Give us this day our daily bread, and forgive us our trespasses as we forgive those who trespass against us.
Lead us not into temptation, but deliver us from evil, for thine is the kingdom, and the power, and the glory, forever. (Matthew 6:9)

Islamic:
Praise be to God, Lord of the universe,
The compassionate, the merciful,
Sovereign of the day of judgment.
You alone we worship, and to You alone we turn for help.
Guide us to the straight path,
The path of those whom You have favored,
Not of those who have incurred Your wrath,
Nor of those who have gone astray. (Koran 1)

Hindu:
May God, who in the mystery of his vision and power
Transforms his white radiance into his many-colored creation,
From whom all things come and into whom they all return,
Grant us the grace of pure vision.
He is the sun, the moon, and the stars.
He is the fire, the waters, and the wind.
He is the creator of all and the Lord of creation. (Svetasvatara Upanishad 4:1)

Taoist:
Tao is beyond words and beyond understanding.
Words may be used to speak of it, but they cannot contain it.
Tao existed before names, before heaven and earth, before the ten thousand things.
It is the unlimited father and mother of all limited things.
Therefore, to see beyond boundaries to the subtle heart of things,
Dispense with names, with concepts, with expectations, ambitions, and differences.
Tao and its many manifestations arise from the same source: subtle wonder within mysterious darkness.
This is the beginning of all understanding. (Tao Te Ching 1)

Buddhist:
Remember the clear light, the pure clear white light from which everything in the universe comes, to which everything in the universe returns, the original nature of your own mind, the natural state of the universe unmanifest.
Let go into the clear light, trust it, merge with it. It is your own true nature, it is home.
The visions you experience exist within your consciousness, the forms they take are determined by your past actions, your past desires, your past fears, your past karma....
Just let them pass through your consciousness like clouds passing through an empty sky. They have no more reality than this.
Remember these teachings, remember the clear light, the pure bright shining white light of your own nature, it is deathless.
If you can look into the visions you can experience and recognize that they are composed of the same pure clear white light as everything else in the universe.
No matter where or how far you wander, the light is only a half-breath away.
It is never too late to recognize the clear light. (Tibetan Book of the Dead)

East and West, Some Parallel Selections

Judaic:

Blessed is the man that walketh not in the counsel of the ungodly, nor standeth in the way of sinners, nor sitteth in the seat of the scornful. But his delight is in the law of the Lord, and in his law doth he meditate day and night. And he shall be like a tree planted by the rivers of water, that bringeth forth his fruit in his season. His leaf also shall not wither, and whatsoever he doeth shall prosper...For the Lord knoweth the way of the righteous, but the way of the ungodly shall perish.(Psalm1)

Taoist:

Whoever is planted in the Tao will not be rooted up. Whoever embraces the Tao will not slip away. Her name will be held in honor from generation to generation. Let the Tao be present in your life, and you will become genuine. Cultivate it in your family, and your family will flourish. Understand it in your country, and your country will be an example to all the countries in the world. Realize it in the universe, and the universe will sing. This I know by looking at the Tao within me. (Tao Te Ching 54)

Christian:

Blessed in spirit are the poor, for theirs is the kingdom of heaven. Blessed are they that mourn, for they shall be comforted. Blessed are the meek, for they shall inherit the earth. Blessed are they which do hunger and thirst after righteousness, for they shall be filled. Blessed are the merciful, for they shall obtain mercy...Let your light so shine before men, that they may see your good works, and glorify your Father which is in heaven. (Matthew 5)

Taoist:

If you hope to expand, you should first contract. If you hope to become strong, you should first weaken yourself. What is ultimately to be discarded must first be embraced. What is ultimately to be taken away, must first be given. This is called the subtle perception of the way things are. The soft overcomes the hard. The slow overcomes the fast. Never abandon the Tao, and the results of your works will be visible. (Tao Te Ching 36)

Judaic:

So Moses went down unto the people and told them God spoke all these words, saying:

1. I am the Lord thy God, who took thee out of the land of Egypt, out of the house of bondage. You shall have no other gods before Me.
2. You shall not make for yourself a graven image, or any likeness which is in the heavens above, which is on the earth below, or which is in the water beneath the earth. You shall not prostrate yourself before them, nor worship them.
3. You shall not take the name of the Lord, your God, in vain.
4. Keep the Sabbath day to sanctify it…Six days may you perform all your labor, but the seventh day is a Sabbath to the Lord your God.
5. Honor your father and your mother, in order that your days be lengthened, and that it may go well with you.
6. You shall not murder.
7. And you shall not commit adultery.
8. And you shall not steal.
9. And you shall not bear false witness against your neighbor.
10. And you shall not covet your neighbor's wife, nor shall you desire your neighbor's house, or anything that belongs to your neighbor. (Exodus 20)

Buddhist:

The Buddha said, I urge you to avoid the ten evils:

1. Do not kill, but have regard for life.
2. Do not steal; but help everybody to be master of the fruits of their labors.
3. Abstain from impurity, and lead a life of chastity.
4. Do not lie, but be truthful. Speak the truth with discretion, fearlessly and in a loving heart.
5. Do not invent evil reports, nor repeat them. Do not find fault, but look for the good sides of your fellow beings.
6. Do not swear, but speak decently and with dignity.
7. Do not waste time with gossip, but speak to the purpose or keep silence.
8. Do not covet, nor envy, but rejoice at the fortunes of other people.
9. Cleanse your heart of malice and cherish no hatred, not even against your enemies; but embrace all living beings with kindness.
10. Free your mind of ignorance and be anxious to learn the truth. Skepticism will make you indifferent and errors will lead you astray, so that you shall not find the noble path that leads to life eternal. (TOB XXIX)

Islamic:

God is the light of the heavens and the earth. His light may be compared to a niche that enshrines a lamp, the lamp within a crystal of star-like brilliance. It is lit from a blessed olive tree neither eastern nor western. Its very oil would almost shine forth, though no fire touched it. Light upon light, God guides to His light whom he will, speaking in metaphors to men, and knowing all things. His light is found in houses which God has sanctioned to be built for the remembrance of His name, where God is glorified in the mornings and the evenings by people who are not diverted by business or commerce from remembrance of God, persistence in prayer, and giving of alms. (Koran 24:35)

Hindu:

There is a Spirit who is awake in our sleep and creates the wonder of dreams. He is Brahman, the Spirit of Light, who in truth is called the Immortal. All the worlds rest on that Spirit and beyond him no one can go...As fire, though one, takes new forms in all things that burn, the Spirit, though one, takes new forms in all things that live...He is the Eternal among things that pass away ...the One who fulfills the prayers of many. Only the wise who see him in their souls attain the peace eternal... Does he give light or does he reflect light? There the sun shines not, nor the moon, the stars, lightning, nor earthly fire. From his light all these give light, and his radiance illumines all creation. (Katha Upanishad 5)

Judaic:

To every thing, there is a season, and a time to every purpose under heaven: a time to be born, a time to die; a time to plant, a time to reap; a time to kill, a time to heal, a time to break down and a time to build up; a time to weep, a time to laugh; a time to mourn, a time to dance; a time to cast away stones, a time to gather stones together; a time to embrace, a time to refrain from embracing; a time to gain, a time to lose; a time to keep, a time to cast away; a time to rend, a time to sew; a time to keep silence, a time to speak; a time to love, a time to hate; a time of war, a time of peace... I know that whatsoever God doeth, it shall be forever: nothing can be put to it, nor any thing taken from it. (Ecclesiastes 3)

Taoist:

If you try to grab hold of the world and do what you want with it, you won't succeed. The world is a vessel for spirit, and it wasn't made to be manipulated. Tamper with it, and you'll spoil it. Hold it, and you'll lose it. There is a time for moving ahead, a time to stay back; a time for being in motion, a time for being at rest; a time to be strong, a time to be weak; a time for rising up, a time for sinking down low; a time to make a great noise, a time to be held silent. The sage sees things as they are, without trying to control them. She lets them go their own way, and resides at the center of the circle. (Tao Te Ching 29)

A Prayer

I sing my thanks for being pervaded with the presence of the One,
Your pleasure passing through the flimsiness of my alleged boundaries,
Granting me strength from the only source of strength,
Joy from the fountain of joy,
And goodness from the essence of what You are, and therefore what I am.
May I impose no barrier, no personal idiocy, to shield some imaginary
separate self from your radiance.
I bask in reverence upon your beach
And ride in exhilaration upon your waves,
In the furtherance of your infinite blessing.

The Purpose

The purpose of meditation and prayer is transcendence. Beyond bodies,
renewing your One-ness with the continuous immortality of the Living
Universe, which some call God, which sends you back to the world with
gifts, yours for the asking.

The Christmas Parable

Three kings kneel before a newborn child.
The baby is holy, bringing Goodness and Light.
We present to him the fruits of our earthly labors,
Vessels of oil, loaves of bread, and gold coins.
For this child, my child, your child
Is the Way, the Truth, the Life,
The incarnation of Infinity, the redeemer,
God's promise of your justification, the new beginning.
Every day a child is born is Christmas Day.
This miracle is before our eyes at all times.

Thousands of Stories

Thousands of stories tell the lives of the holy ones to whom we look for guidance and example. I shall send no team of experts to verify their miracles. For it has been revealed unto me, the metaphor is the message.

Dragged by men into the courtrooms of materialistic science, are the scriptures that will no longer connect those men to Infinity. Subject to verification by the game-rules of an intricately constellated world, these teachings have been compromised, lowered to meaninglessness under the scrutiny of the literal mind.

It's been told that some graduate student with lab coat and clipboard has successfully analyzed wave vibrations and produced a mathematical formula for the sound of one hand clapping. O, the insipidness of the surface-dwellers!

Seek instead the inner statement, which speaks to the inner Self, the One, whom you really are! Certainly in sacred writings you must permit the imagery to pull back the shroud of ignorance, solidity, and factuality.

And even in the mundane messages as Let's do the laundry, seek the rendition consecrating your actions and thoughts to your oneness with your Source. For the secret is that every communication, impulse, action, and object in this dream we call the world, is but a metaphor of God.

Woman, Thou Art Mary

Know ye not that I speak in parables?
I am the Way as You are the Way,
As you are the Truth and the Life.

To learn my ways, look to the baby,
The purity of responses not yet ushered
From the Garden to thy fallen world.

Woman, thou art Mary. And every child
Thou bearest is begotten of God
And in his ways find ye thy salvation.

Born innocent into a pristine world
He learneth from you of good and evil
And the wilderness between, he must traverse.

Thou wilt teach to him thy ways
To see not the world created by God
Which He didst pronounce six times good.

Instead thou teachest thy relative world.
Forget ye not my parables of thy child and thyself,
For you are the Way, the Truth and the Life.

The Least of the Jesi

Knock knock. Who's there? Jesus. Jesus who? The historical Jesus. The hysterical Jesus? To him I'd like to speak. No, the historical Jesus. Ah, the impostor, least of the Jesi, the finite concept in dashboard statuary. Bring me instead the magical mystery bread, and the metaphorical wine, the communion of Father and Son.

To Worship As We Choose

We come to this beach today to worship as we choose,
To sit this Sunday morning, close to the great ocean.
As I silently chant my mantra, it is not just I who knows.
Facing the waves, watching for something inward,
As the surfer awaits his appointed wave in secret wisdom
That this is his opportunity to pursue his truest self.

We come to this bed tonight to worship as we choose,
This night, with you, for whom so fervently I prayed,
Each night of my boyhood, in the ancient rhythmic prayer,
In partnership with God, to bring you into existence.
From glimpses, glances, photos, and dreams we designed you,
The altar of love, who guides me to my own perfect self.

Truth Must Reconcile

The Creation really happened or it didn't. The Separation is God's will or
it isn't. Individuality, ego, a relative world, and human limitations are real
or imagined.
Is it a wave or a particle? Truth must reconcile: In the mind of God, all the
opposites are understood without conflict.
Let us go there.

A Simple Catechism

Do you see God? You see only God. There is nothing else but illusions and
nightmares.

What would I tell her if I were her minister? You are her minister. That is
why it is you who happens to be there at this moment.

Why Let There Be Light?

These are the metaphors, these stories of the creation, of the One (you) becoming the Many (still you). And by the use of great force of mind successfully pretending for an instant, for just a split second forgetting that you are the One. Entertaining the idea, just for a moment, the preposterous idea that there are entities who can perceive themselves as separate.

It is so utterly impossible, that the concept cannot be held. In the very moment of its conception the obvious One-ness of all washes the thought-game away. So why do it? Why would a boundless Being enforce a shattered array of separate viewpoints?

Why? For the pleasure of the glorification of Truth, as when you play peek-a-boo with a very small child. "Where is she? Where is she? Oh! There she is! There she is!" What joy for both in finding whom you had never really lost! Every instant of your human existence is this same game of peek-a-boo with your own real Identity. And the brief instant of self-generated unknowingness can be perceptually expanded to appear as an entire lifetime with many adventures, because thoughts do not take up space or time.

Kazantzakis' Jesus of "The Last Temptation of Christ," after a compellingly realistic dream of an entire average life, awakens on the cross, relieved that he didn't duck away from his destiny. And Captain Picard of Star Trek experiences a full lifetime of domestic fulfillment and civic service, only to awaken on the Enterprise with no time elapsed. Why are these tales so haunting?

Upon your re-cognition of the One, you see that none of the alleged adventures really happened. "There she is!" What we experience as thousands of years of human history, countless births and deaths and the emotional thrill-ride of each life, are less than the blink of an eye, a fleeting "What if...." of the higher Self.

All your muscular efforts, electrical energy, nuclear power and other physical forces that light your homes, run your machinery, and kill your enemies, all the energy in the world, comes from the mental effort of pretending to be unaware of the One.

Past Lives

Seventy-seven pseudo messiahs, currently under twenty-four hour care, each claiming to be the reincarnated Jesus. They can't all be right, can they? Or can they?

Could those past lives, all those billions of lives be yours? Jesus, Napoleon, the whole gang, all you? Perhaps they aren't in the past at all, unless you happen to file them in a folder with such a temporarily convenient label.

With effort you've separated from some of these identities, and see them outside yourself, as historical icons, friends and acquaintances, enemies and extras, in this game of fractured life, assigning portions of your Greater Self to other times or places.

The World You See

Suppose the world you see, and every person you meet, and everything you seem to do are but a metaphor for the God you worship, a metaphor for your vision of what you are.

The next song you hear, your next response to the person in front of you, and tomorrow's weather would be part of the parable you composed, to publish in matter the truths you find real.

Your allies and your enemies, your teachers and your tormentors, your lovers, friends, husbands, wives, children, even your parents as you know them, and an endless cast of extras were selected as the perfect players in the drama of your long and winding journey to Infinity, the place you never left.

If the beauty, the terror, and the glory of all your constellations, the world as you know it, is a metaphor, then Who are You really?

Made In Heaven

There is a designer label of woven fabric just inside the back of your neck. The same label, sewn with strands of light, is affixed to your soul. It's on every leaf of every tree, the waves of the ocean, all of existence large or small, even under your coffee table. It reads "Made in Heaven, 100% God."

Farewell Magdalena

For the radiant goddess of the desert, Magdalena Bas Ibrahim, whose approach brings the sunrise and all the colors to the sky, it is as it has been before and shall be ever and ever again: a last intimate moment with her beloved, Yeshu the Nazarene, before the surrender to duty sets an inevitable destiny into motion.

He who for her is the prophet, the voice, the *bashert*, the savior, who is her way, her truth, and her life, the answer to both her passion for the world and her yearning for heaven, lives forever inside her as a promise from Ha-Shem.

We shall meet again, he says, for as long as the world exists, its very existence depends upon you and I coming together, as do the earth and the heaven, yin and yang.

You and I, my love, in all times and all places, now and forever, through many disguises, in the unlikeliest lands and impossible coincidences, cast together to recognize again the secret self, and thereby shall the world be renewed by our joining, for the celebration and the glory of that from which we never were apart.

Bibliography

The following editions have been referenced for scriptural quotes.

The Torah, trans. Jewish Publication Society, Labyrinth Publishing
ArtScroll Siddur, trans. Rabbi Nosson Scherman, Mesorah Publications
Holy Bible, King James Version, Oral Roberts Evangelistic Association
A Course In Miracles, Foundation for Inner Peace
The Koran, trans. N. J. Dawood, Penguin Classics
The Essential Koran, trans. Thomas Cleary, Castle Books
The Bhagavad Gita, trans. Swami Prabhavananda, Mentor Religious Classics
The Bhagavad Gita, trans. Juan Mascaro, Penguin Classics
The Upanishads, trans. Juan Mascaro, Penguin Classics
A Vedic Reader, trans. Arthur Anthony Macdonell, D. K. Publications
The Way of Life, ed. Witter Bynner, Capricorn Books
The Tao Te Ching, trans. Brian Browne Walker, St. Martin's Press
Loa Tzu, trans. Cheng Man Ching, North Atlantic Books
The Complete Works of Lao Tzu, trans. Hua-Ching Ni, Seven Star
The Tao Te Ching, trans. Stephen Mitchell, Perennial Classics
Hua Hu Ching, trans. Brian Browne Walker, Harper Collins
The I Ching, trans. Rudolf Ritsema and Stephen Karcher, Barnes and Noble
The I Ching, trans. R. Wilhelm and Cary F. Baynes, Princeton University Press
The Teachings of Buddha (TOB), ed. Paul Carus, St. Martin's Press
Teachings of the Buddha (TTB), ed. Jack Kornfield, Shambhala Publications
The Tibetan Book of the Dead, trans. Robert Thurman, Bantam Books
The Tibetan Book of the Dead, ed. W.Y. Evans-Wentz, Oxford University Press
Dhammapada, The Way of Truth, trans. Sangharakshita, Barnes and Noble
The Dhammapada, ed. Anne Bancroft, Vega

This is dedicated to my beloved wife, Cathy, the dream-angel from earlier existences, upon whom the Magdalena character was designed, and without whom the mystical conjunction of solar and lunar plexus, the resurrection implicit in crucifixion, and the dark liqueurs distilled from the nexus of joy and pain, would be mere theories.

About the Author

Mark Dobson graduated from Brooklyn College in literature and philosophy, with additional post-graduate studies in world religions and religious practices, serving as a minister for seventeen years. His articles on common threads amongst the faiths, and the prophetic relevance of popular music, have appeared in *Tai Chi* and *The Lightworker*. He lives in central Florida with his wife, Cathy, where he designs and builds playgrounds and tree houses.

Printed in the United States
22141LVS00005B/382-408